W9-CAA-051

Your Other Self

by CANON JEAN VIEUJEAN, *Professor of Religious Sciences, University of Louvain, Belgium*

Translated from the French by RICHARD E. CROSS

The Newman Press · 1959 · *Westminster, Maryland*

This is a translation of *L'Autre Toi-même* published by Éditions Casterman, Paris and Tournai.

Nihil obstat: EDWARD A. CERNY, S.S., D.D.   *Imprimatur:* FRANCIS P. KEOUGH, D.D.
Censor Librorum   *Archbishop of Baltimore*

July 15, 1958

The *nihil obstat* and *imprimatur* are official declarations that a book or pamphlet is free of doctrinal and moral error. No implication is contained therein that those who have granted the *nihil obstat* and *imprimatur* agree with the opinions expressed.

Contents

Introduction

LIFE with one's fellow human beings could be a paradise.
But it is often a purgatory.
At times, even, it is hell.
Many people, whether they be in an office, a factory, or
a school, really live a life of solitude in common. They live,
eat, and work together, but they hardly commune with one
another. Their souls remain walled up in solitude.
This same phenomenon is found in many families. A
woman once told Dr. Tournier: "My husband seems like
a mysterious isle which I encircle endlessly without ever
finding a beach on which I can land."
Today, men have become keenly aware of this moral
isolation. They have been forced to realize that it isn't
enough to create societies or organizations whose mecha-
nisms are geared to perfection. At least some have begun to
realize more and more that a soul must be put back in all
those groups in which men live together.
Should we despair of succeeding in this? Are we really
at "the twenty-fifth hour"—an hour too late? Have men
all over the world gone to such extremes that there is little
hope for a solution, that "even the coming of a Messias
would solve nothing, since a technocratic society cannot
create spirit, and therefore has turned to creating monsters"?

Such pessimism is understandable in those who have had to live under oppression in the past, or who are oppressed even today in many parts of the world. But the intensity of suffering can make our fears unwarranted. For no matter what has happened in the past or what may happen again, there will come an hour when "God will have pity on man as He has done so often before."

We must prepare for this hour. This is why we should welcome with joy all those who constantly remind our world of its need to give a heart and soul to human society, and, by so doing, re-create living communities. Men like Péguy, Carrel, Thibon, Simone Weil, and Saint Exupéry will always be remembered in this regard. These and so many others are the "gifts that Providence never fails to give in troubled times."

There has also been much activity in the form of "social work." Its main purpose should be, not so much to render any determined service or to unravel the entanglement of social laws, but rather to help men and organizations find the soul they have lost. Social work ought to strive to give them a heart that is attentive to all human needs. What threatens this work most is that it can become one more machine among machines! And this danger will only be avoided by vigilance.

Generous souls often dedicate all their energy in launching some vast movement in the world to re-create relations between individuals and groups. They would have these relations sealed with loyalty, respect, cordiality, justice, sincerity, and altruism. Such is the Christopher Movement founded by Father Keller.

Philosophers themselves are concerned over the salvation of mankind. The best among them, in spite of their differences of opinion, praise fellowship, love, and charity as the only means for a human being to realize himself and foster his growth and development.

Finally, many unassuming authors strive to spread the same ideas in articles and books. Such a man is the Swiss doctor, Paul Tournier. His life's work has been inspired by this same ideal: to restore the notion of true community life.

Surely those whom Christ commanded to announce His message of charity have never failed in their mission. Yet, they have, perhaps, confined themselves too exclusively to principles, theories, and theological considerations. On the other hand, it would surely be another excess to be content with such methods as those of Carnegie in his famous little book, *How to Win Friends and Influence People.* For although some of them show a real concern for one's neighbor, the ensemble has something artificial about it. Far from being the outpouring of an authentic and disinterested charity, it is rather (and the author doesn't try to hide it) a manual for "succeeding in life."

Wouldn't we find the ideal, rather, in the formation of a living and active spirit—a spirit that is in contact with what is concrete and commonplace, yet considered in all its depth and mystery? This is what this book would like to do. It aspires to stay simple, practical, down to earth, and in contact with daily reality. Yet, it wants as well to plunge deep into the hidden folds of man's heart. It even would like to approach the mystery of God sometimes, for here is the real source of every community. Hasn't God defined Himself as Charity, as Love? Isn't the Blessed Trinity the first and most living of all communities? Isn't It the origin and exemplar of all others?

It may happen that you will be seized with fear in the

face of some of Charity's demands: "Must I really go *that* far in loving my neighbor?"

Yes. That far! Love him *as yourself*. Christ has said it. But we must go even farther! He asks that we love others as *He* loves them.

Oh, we won't get there in one day. We may never get there. But, we ought to aim there, with the help of His grace. We ought to give our all each day . . . knowing all the while that our all is never *really* our all!

We may feel we are even "losing our soul." But some day we shall see that it is only in losing it that we really find it. For nothing creates persons like love.

Your Other Self

1. *The Grandeur of Love*

THERE is no greater power than love—whether it be good or bad. Nothing takes on such diverse aspects or such opposite perspectives: "cheerful and sad, ardent and disheartened, sublime and pathetic." Nothing falls more easily into corruption, baseness, or morbidity. But when it is purified and lived in its human and divine fulness, there is no richer source of internal peace, perfection in our neighbor, or social cohesion.

Men often distort the meaning of love, because they look at it from only one viewpoint. Each one wants to reduce it to the scope of his particular science or his own life. Psychiatrists can see in it only a criminal drive of disequilibrium, for their only interest is in its perverted manifestations: jealousy, hate, vanity, and vengeance. Biologists have reduced it to a simple sex-attraction that is merely a physico-chemical phenomenon. Psychologists and novelists mainly see in it the instinct of sympathy, and the host of dramas to which it gives rise because of its instability. Even our moralists and theologians have considered it too exclusively, perhaps, from the spiritual and supernatural side.

Love that is worthy of man is above all an intimate communion with another's true person. It is seizing him spiritually in his most intimate self, in his own mystery, in the throbbing of his personality, in his unique destiny, and in his absolute value.

It is touching, feeling, tasting, and savouring the intimate reality of another. It is entering within him, identifying ourself with him, coinciding with him. It is experiencing him as another self, and, therefore, being willing to protect him, perfect him, gladden him, develop him, create him, make him become something.

This creative force must be found in all true human love, whether it be conjugal, parental, filial, the love of friendship, or even that of authentic social relations. Without doubt it will take on various intensities and colorings. But it will always imply this profound meeting of two persons, or else it will run the risk of staying beneath what is truly human.

But man is not a pure spirit. He is also a commingling of sentiments, passions, and instincts. It isn't surprising, then, to find love rising up from our feelings. This is called the instinct of sympathy, sensible love, or the passion of love.

Most of us think of this sentiment as soon as we hear the word *love* pronounced. Some find charm and poetry in it. They imagine the wave of joy that surges in the heart and makes it beat faster, radiating itself throughout the whole being, brightening the eyes, and parting the lips with a smile.

Others dream of its varying power: at one moment kind, at another destructive. Today it may be the font of all sincerity, dignity, modesty, fervor, confidence, generosity, and heroism. But tomorrow it may well become a crater erupting with the lava of folly, weakness, egoism, guile, blindness, vileness, suspicion, insipidness, hatred, chaos, cruelty, and madness.

Others are tempted to make of it a god that is at once

sovereign, despotic, and invincible, and to whom all rights must be conceded. The very idea that love ought to be governed, and sometimes even combatted, shocks their spirit as if an outrage were being committed against the human person.

Of course, sensible love is a great force and we must not make light of it. But, like all human instincts, it is a blind drive. We must never for an instant dream of destroying it. Each one of us should keep within him a vivid and keen sensitivity that is prompt to be moved and inflamed. But we must never surrender or abandon ourselves to it nor delight in it. We must educate this powerful sentiment all our life, purify, dominate, and guide it. Sometimes the struggle can be so great that one dies from it, but at least he has behaved like an intelligent and free being. When passionate love decomposes a person, breaks up a family, or ruins a vocation, it deserves but one name: enemy—an evil to be opposed mercilessly.

Man is a corporal being. "I am not just a soul," says St. Thomas. I am a being composed of body and soul. Now love seizes the *whole* man, body as well as soul. The incarnate spirit that I am cannot manifest, express, or communicate itself except through the body. We need signs to reveal ourselves to others. The most spiritual friendship imaginable has need of a word, a look, a smile, a handshake. Maternal love gives and craves caresses. And married love expresses itself by the total abandonment of the couple to each other.

There is, then, a physical aspect to love. We shall point out later on how this participation of bodies in the communion of persons can be the source of the most tragic misunderstandings that can arise in love.

Words and gestures manifest souls, but at the same time

they conceal them. These gestures can easily become routine and mechanical habits. They no longer express the spirit then; they are no longer "charged with soul"; they become meaningless rituals. In other instances (and this is the menace that hovers over the closest of all unions, that of man and wife) the physical element tends to become autonomous, separated from the spiritual, and self-seeking in its own pleasure.

There is only one way to escape this crisis: to nourish within us a spiritual life so intense that it spontaneously pervades our person in all its acts and integrates our body more and more perfectly into its own impulse. For our body has value only because of the spirit that animates it.

What we have just said is especially true of conjugal love. More than any other, this love unites a couple in a communion that engages their person in all its mystery. By the same fact, it is one of the gravest acts a man and a woman can perform.

"If the union of man and woman is the fruit of a love that is given in purity, generosity, and fidelity, then the body itself is spiritualized in the service of a love that enobles it, and, with God's blessing, sanctifies. Then man remains man, that is to say, flesh sustained by spirit. If the union is the issue of an instinct devoid of generosity, of a gift made without purity, of an attraction involving no fidelity, then the soul itself is abased, degraded, gradually reduced to the same level of carnality and animality as the love that drags it down: and the man, thus fallen beneath himself, becomes no more than a spirit miserably fettered to the senses." [1]

Purify love. Spiritualize it. This is one of the most im-

[1] Jean Mouroux, *The Meaning of Man,* translated by A. H. G. Downes (New York: Sheed & Ward, Inc., 1948).

portant aspects of man's vocation. It is a work of charity,
loyalty, and good will. This alone can save love from all
the distortions, corruptions, and disgraces that constantly
threaten it. This alone can lead it toward a perfection that,
here on earth, is the most beautiful reflection of God's own
perfection. For God *is* love.

2. *Loving in God*

Is rr possible that we put our Lord's instructions into
practice so badly that the expression "working out of love
for God" has come to mean working without impulse, fervor,
warmth, or love? Are all those people right who think the
phrase "loving in God" means loving without real love,
loving yet staying all the while indifferent to the one we
pretend to love? What a paradox!

One person who made this mistake was a nun, Sister
Lucile, who was also a nurse. So unfortunate as to lack a few
"essentials" in the realm of the intelligence, as well as in
the realm of the heart, she was completely dry as far as
feelings were concerned. Unhappily her Mother Superior
was hardly more intelligent, and she often cited Sister Lucile
as an example of "those who know how to put themselves
above what is human, and how to care for the sick . . . on the
spiritual level. That is: being completely detached from the
life, sickness, suffering, or health of those over whom
Providence watches." [1]

[1] Etienne de Greeff, *La nuit est ma lumière* (Paris: Editions du Seuil, 1949).

No one would dream of denying it! It happens only too often that people misunderstand the demands of supernatural love, of charity. They think that "to love God" means to see Him only and to forget His creatures, to consider the human person with indifference. Only then, they feel, will their love be pure and truly supernatural.

The regime of such equivocations must be overthrown!

Of course, supernatural love demands a certain indifference, but only in the sense that we favor no one in particular: each man has the right to our sincere and fraternal welcome, whether he be rich or poor, mighty or lowly, intelligent or stupid, good or bad.

Of course, too, supernatural love should be detached, but not in the sense that we should have no interest in people; rather in the sense that we do not love them for our own interests and out of pure selfishness. One of the loveliest qualities of love is that it is given freely and purely, stripped of all self-love. Perhaps we will never arrive at such perfection, but we must tirelessly strive after it, or else our love will tend more and more toward egotism and become merely self-centered passion.

However, forgetting ourself is not the same as forgetting another. Detachment means that we do not make an absolute of our beloved. To do so would be to draw the curtain on God and turn our backs on Him. Nor does detachment mean that we become disinterested in another's person, his life, his feelings, his sufferings. Nor does it mean that we look upon him as an impersonal "X," as a thing, or an occasion to prove our love for God.

Simone Weil has rightly said that "God is not present, even if we invoke Him, where the afflicted are merely regarded as an occasion for doing good."

Loving God implies, includes, and demands above all a real and sincere love of my neighbor, and an engaging of my being in behalf of his being.

Etienne de Greeff describes very well the evolution from abstract to concrete love, which is the only kind worthy of the name, for "love is not real unless it is directed toward a particular object":

Sister Colette entered the convent after breaking off a proposed marriage. Now a turn of events led her to have the care of her former fiancé's wife, Elizabeth, who had lost her mind.

At first, Sister Colette considered Elizabeth solely as a patient, and even a little as a rival. But once, in a momentary spell of lucidity, the young woman confided in the nun with complete abandonment and touching delicacy. Sympathy and affection for the sick woman suddenly flooded the soul of Sister Colette. Elizabeth ceased to be a stranger, an abstraction. She became "Elizabeth."

"It was like a ray of sunshine piercing a thick, gray cloud and suddenly illuminating everything. Sister Colette herself was amazed at the purity and completeness of her sympathy, at the absolute concern she had for Maurice's wife."

That evening, she wrote these significant words:

"Lord, thank You for this day. I think I have caught a glimpse of one of the possible meanings of my life. Until now, I cared for the sick, especially those here, without ever realizing that a disease is something superficial, an accidental state of being.

"Without a doubt, I was not unaware of this, yet I never really knew to what extent it was true. . . .Today, however, when I had that talk, that real contact with Elizabeth, I felt the futility of my reasoning until then. . . . I felt, in the presence of her anguish, that my being should share, and that it actually was sharing in it wholly and entirely. . . . It is to this giving that I must remain faithful; it must be my moral rule. No longer will I act for abstract brethren, or devote myself to a theoretical humanity, to unknown friends whom I would like to save, without even taking the trouble to know them. . . .

"Tonight, I suddenly learned that I had never really committed myself to anyone else. . . . These people I have been wanting to save, to tear away from barbarity and paganism, to help—these have been only abstract forms to me. I never really went out of myself before; I never had the revelation of another. . . .

"Until now, I looked upon others as my inferiors. I wanted to offer and give myself, but in so doing I wanted to be conscious of the fact that I was above them. All in all, my charity was really a form of dominating others; and my devotion and sacrifice were but affirmations of myself. . . .

"Today, I understood all this as Elizabeth spoke to me. When I suddenly perceived her soul, I realized exactly what a human soul really is, what a destiny and a life can be. It was a luminous revelation for me, a grace that I feel is here to stay, for I suddenly felt myself unimportant and became completely engaged in saving her, in protecting her as whole-heartedly as a mother protects her child. For a moment, I completely forgot myself; and in so doing I shared myself with another. . . ." [2]

There is no true love, no authentic charity, without this discovery. Every human being ought to be considered and loved in the unique mystery of his concrete personality.

[2] de Greeff, *op. cit.*

"Loving in God" presupposes this above all else. And so Sister Colette was right when she added: "I also think, my God, that I must have been very close to You, that I had a share in Your charity, and that I at last understood what You want of me."

There is something else, however, that charity takes for granted other than this discovery of the concrete reality of a human person. More exactly, charity goes beyond it: it plunges deeper into this reality. It penetrates as far as the hidden mystery of the being before it. And this mystery is God: the real presence of God in this person.

This being before me offers itself for my love; it is not just Peter, James, or Joseph, with his body and soul, his own self. No. This is a creature of God, a being fettered to God by an eternal bond of total dependency, for he is a being in whom God works and whom God sustains. He is a being with whom God is very intimate, even more so than he is with himself. Such a man is inseparably united to his creator. To see him united to God, and in His presence, is to see him as he truly is: apart from God, he cannot be really known.

Futhermore, we know that man has been redeemed by Christ and that God has desired to knit a relationship between Himself and man even closer than that of creator and creature. God's wish is to make man His child. He has given him His own life, communicated to him the most secret thing He has. And He realizes this union with man by an unutterable presence, a mysterious and gratuitous indwelling that makes us one with Him, with His life, and His indescribable joy.

"Loving in God" is seeing man enveloped in this love. Even when he does not possess God by grace, because of some obstacle he has put in the way, he still remains eligible for divine love, a saint by aspiration. At no instant, and in no case, must we forget this vocation, this divine destiny that is man's.

Love becomes charity precisely when it perceives, recognizes, and loves God thus present in man, and man thus present in the bosom of God. Here we are not replacing man with God, but looking upon man and loving him in his most living reality, in his most sacred mystery. Here we see man at the center of the Love Who created him, sustains him, and communicates Himself to him.

Charity, moreover, is to love with God present in our own heart, to participate in God's own charity, to love with the very love God puts in our heart.

Charity is a true love, then, real and concrete. It is a greater and higher love. When we "love in God," we evoke and reach the deepest sense of any human being. It is a love in which God takes part by giving His Heart to the one loving, and His countenance to the one loved.

Charity is more than a man who loves: it is God loving with him and in him. And it is more than a mere man who is loved; it is a man who is God-like, or who at least can be so. It is a man loved with the love of God, redeemed by the blood of God, and inhabited by the very life of God.

If man would only realize that it is really he who is loved, when we speak of "loving in God"! It is his own self that we love, his elevated self, transfigured by God, and so God-like that a mere gaze reflects the adorable countenance of God and fills us with religious awe as we approach him.

3. *Solitude in Common*

IN THE first of three short stories published under the
title of *Solitudes,* Édouard Estaunié introduces an old maid,
Mademoiselle Gauche, who has lived alone since she was
eighteen, glued to her armchair. . . .

"But," she says, "one is not alone when he has prayer
and memories as I have. I never cease praying or dreaming
of the past. This is enough to distract me. Never sad, never
gay. . . . A grey sky is a sky nonetheless. . . ."

Then one day, a distant nephew arrives, making a display of his affection, but really only aspiring to an inherit-
ance. The old maid's heart takes a new leap. But soon the
nephew goes away and allows her letters to remain un-
answered.

Then, Mademoiselle Gauche becomes so vividly conscious
of her solitude that she dies. . . .

Is it prudent to speak of solitude in a book that wants to
cure men of it?

The solitude in question here is not mere physical isolation, but rather a phenomenon that is essential to man's
condition as a human being. Whatever he may do, or whatever anyone may do for him, man lives alone and dies alone.
There is a radical inability in him to communicate himself
to others to the depths of his personality, and it is likewise

impossible for him to penetrate to the last hidden fold of another's being. For there is in each man a secret region that cannot be conveyed to another, that cannot be reached by another. No one can see the hidden soul that lives behind the soul he does see. "No one will ever reach the knowledge of a single human soul; it is the secret of each one—an interior country, with virgin plains, silent ravines, and hidden paradises."

Solitude, then, is a universal evil. Yet this sentiment is deaf and dormant in many of us. It dwells in our marginal consciousness and is confused with the desire for something else, the waiting for a tomorrow, the hope that the coming hour will bring the happiness that the previous hour has refused. This sentiment penetrates our consciousness only under the shock of exterior events, as in the case mentioned above; or it can happen that age and experience gradually illuminate the innermost states of our profound self.

Should we not do all we can to keep this sudden awareness away from men, since such a discovery may be fatal? Is this not exposing men to evil's contagion rather than pointing it out?

We do not think so. Since the evil exists, we must regard it objectively. This is behaving like a man. We should realize that this evil is partially incurable here below, but that it can be surmounted. We can employ it as a higher moral perfection, and find in it the application of a very resolute gift of self to others and to God.

The sentiment of solitude essentially comes from the fact that man is a spiritual and personal being, a nucleus, an absolute set in the face of other absolutes: men and God. When a man becomes intensely conscious of himself, he grasps himself as an isolated world, linked to other beings,

but possessing nonetheless an existence, in a certain autonomous way, that is proper to himself. He feels himself
free, entrusted to himself, and responsible for his own
destiny. No one can decide for him, nor would he ever allow
anyone to try. This intuition of his freedom is one of the
factors that produces a very keen awareness of his absolute
metaphysical solitude.

Many, especially the young, imagine that their solitude
will find an outlet sometime, and will come to an end. They
especially think of that sister soul in whom they will be able
to confide entirely and who will keep no secret from them.
This is a dangerous illusion, against which we must dis-
cretely warn them.

"Wedlock," writes Dr. Allers, "seems to be the image of
union *par excellence* here on earth. There is no intimacy
and communion between human beings more immediate
or profound. But this union still leaves something to be
desired. It still does not realize that identity of two beings,
that desire to be received into another, such as love imagines
it. Whatever they may do, there can be no melting of the
one into the other." Further on he adds: "Even nuptial love,
the greatest intimacy that one being can have with another,
never allows a person to reach the supreme depth of another's
self, nor to open to another the most hidden sources of one's
own being." [1]

Man's deep solitude is also explained by the fact that he
is both spiritual and corporal. "What solitude these human
bodies are!" said Pascal.

Our condition here below is truly a paradox. Souls cannot communicate with one another without the body. Words,
looks, and gestures are our only means of entering into

[1] R. Allers, *L'amour et l'instinct.*

relation with others—our only means of becoming present to them and participating in their intimate life. A direct communion of spirits does not exist on earth. Yet, at the same time the body unites, it also separates and isolates; it remains as a screen between souls.

It can even happen that it is nothing more than a means of separation: "Such division can be set up between two workmen toiling at the same bench, between parent and child, between husband and wife: associations made for communion, bodies which touch, collaborate, even inter-mingle, and souls that turn away in refusal. What wonder, then, if this lifeless presence of bodies to each other, this real absence in enforced presence, should turn in the end to hate, and shatter every remaining semblance of living community?" [2]

Well, then, is there nothing left but to despair?

Not at all!

But, above all, we must *accept*. We must sincerely reconcile ourselves to the finite and imperfect character of our human condition. How many friends, and especially how many married couples, have raised havoc with their union because they did not have the *courage of imperfection!* They were looking for an absolute, and found only what was relative. Thinking they had the wrong number, they were naive enough to hope that they would quench their thirst for absolute intimacy elsewhere. They shattered possible happiness to follow a chimera, whereas, in accepting their limitations, they would have seen their union grow deeper each day and become the source of an endlessly growing happiness.

If only people understood this! To accept does not mean

[2] Jean Mouroux, *The Meaning of Man.*

to fold our arms or let them fall at our sides. We must continually strive to surpass ourselves, to go beyond our body. If we wish people to meet and communicate more intimately with one another, it is not to the body that we must turn. Émile Verhaeren wrote to his wife: "If there is no soul behind kisses, it is hardly worth the trouble to go toward each other, so finite is the flesh."

We must look to the spirit. It is the soul that we must make more clear, loyal, pure, detached, and crystalline. Then it will reclothe our words, eyes, gestures, and bodies with its light. It will see others more clearly and at the same time become more transparent to them. "In true love," writes Nietzsche, "it is the soul that envelops the body."

Above all, we must see others rather than ourselves.

In the third story of *Solitudes*, Édouard Estaunié introduces a young couple who seem to have everything necessary for their happiness. Soon, however, Peter, the husband, realizes that "behind the soul that is his delight sleep other souls that escape him," and that if he can never attain the fulness of the gift, it will neither be the fault of his appeal nor the fault of his wife's good will. "I am continually obsessed," he says, "by the idea that we are two, she and I."

Were he wise, he would accept it. But he is not resigned and so the drama is intensified. When he can no longer bear it, he goes to see a priest to tell him his troubles and seek a remedy.

". . . It is very easy," said the priest; "take refuge in God. Be convinced that you ought to love Him only, and, in loving Him alone, experience such detachments on earth that your troubles will gradually cease to exist. . . ."

But Peter is an unbeliever. He angrily answers that he

has not come for mystical remedies and asks him to give him an answer that excludes a faith in which he has no part.

". . . In that case," continues the priest, "it is also very simple: do nothing! What you judge to be an extraordinary case, dear sir, is rather the general rule. You are undergoing an evolution that is common. For some years, now, you have dreamed of realizing a total fusion of your two beings into one soul. . . . It's too bad that you counted on escaping the norm ruling all humanity. . . . Man is alone, necessarily alone."

Later, however, the priest is a little more encouraging. He says to Peter: "My friend, it isn't enough just to know solitude. Once you have realized that one plus one always remain two, without ever becoming one, then you must go beyond: forget one of the unities, yourself, I mean, and think about the other. Sacrifice does not call for great shouting or sublime gestures. It is an act much humbler, more down to earth, if you will. It consists in building peace in another's heart with bits of your own, in ceasing to be shocked afterwards at having won by yourself, and by a roundabout way, a tranquillity which you no longer believed in."

He who forgets himself finds himself; he who gives, receives; he who loses himself, finds himself!

Jacques Leclercq writes: "Human friendship and human love can go a long way toward union: but not 'all the way,' for God reserves this 'all the way' to Himself. Human love can only be perfectly harmonious if we accept it as it is— powerless to give all; if we yield to the fact that there is something beyond, the part reserved for God, and if we coordinate it to this part reserved for God, in seeking to make of the love itself a means of coming closer to God." [3]

There are only two outlets from solitude: our neighbor and God. And we will escape it completely only in heaven.

The sentiment of solitude is God's signature on man's heart. It is the infallible sign that we do not have our completion here below and that we are made for a homeland where hearts will penetrate each other, having remained hidden from each other so long: where souls will be totally transparent to one another in God's own light, God Himself having also become transparent.

One of Estaunié's characters says: "If solitude is the essence of life, why shouldn't death be the access to a land where one is never alone?"

4. *Humble Love*

ORIENTALS love to speak about humble love. They have made it the basis of their spirituality.

Just what is humble love?

It is love that has become the first and total inspiration of all the soul's animation—love that is not just practiced because God commands it, but rather a love that has become the very substance of life, the soul's very breathing.

It is a love that discretion, humility, modesty, and forgetfulness of self bathe in an unparalleled light. It is a love in which we not only respect, but kneel in adoration.

[3] *Dialogue de l'homme et de Dieu.*

This love is not afraid of humiliation. It doesn't cry out: "My dignity! My personality! My value! My prestige!" Its care is only for the good of others. And it embraces all God's creatures, even those deprived of reason, for there, as well, one touches God. Everything is sacred and has a share in the divine mystery: the sea, the mountains, the storm, the forest, the tiny flower in the field, and those little brothers of ours, the birds.

But this love is especially directed to man, for here it venerates the image and likeness of God. He who is animated by this love first of all respects himself, his own proper mystery, his own vocation, and the idea God has of him. He also acts with immense respect toward others, judging no one: not pretending to take the speck out of his neighbor's eye and forgetting the beam in his own. He mistrusts craftiness, constraint, even his own power, and is quite content to stimulate the resources hidden in his neighbor's liberty. Yet he is no milquetoast; rather he is full of boldness, for defeat does not frighten him. Despite its apparent weakness, humble love is a gigantic force.

Nothing disarms hostile hearts like humble love. Charles Sylvestre beautifully illustrates this idea: Monica sees her husband being led farther and farther away from his home by two adventurers who are only interested in his money. She is quite aware that any interference on her part would be futile, for her husband is of a violent disposition, and in his eyes she hardly exists, for he has not yet understood the forces that lies hidden in her gentleness. She humbly stays near, yet never letting her husband think she is deceived or consents to evil. There is never a reproach in her words or attitude, but her whole life is a clear and discreet appeal for that wholesome Christian life which her unbelieving husband once knew.

Moreover, she spends her spare time relieving the physical and moral miseries about her.

Here is one episode that clearly shows the power of her humble love: Germaine, a young girl from a neighboring village, returned from Paris "so dissipated in body and soul that her parents had great fear of her endless blaspheming and vile speech." Monica had suffered her insults more than once.

"One day as Monica was passing near the squalid house, Germaine broke into an offensive and dirty song, whose refrains could be stuffed with impurity at will, for they had as much elasticity as the accordions accompanying them. For a moment Monica was struck by an obstinate, blinding despair. Recalling all the injuries she had borne in vain, she was about to turn away, murmuring, 'My God, I don't want . . .' Suddenly she heard the old mother crying at the top of her voice: 'I'm ashamed of you, street-walker, wretch. Shut up!'

"Germaine retorts, trembling with emotion: 'Don't worry! . . . I'll go drown myself soon . . . and it'll be no loss to you or me.' Monica stiffened. . . . She couldn't go away after hearing such a dangerous cry. . . . Perhaps God had allowed her to be struck by it. . . . She was searching for words to say, and found nothing—none of those words that have wings powerful and mysterious enough to reach the most hidden hearts, the most lost. Before knocking at the door, she felt she had not been humble enough. Then, coughing to let her approach be known, she knocked at the worm-eaten door and stood in the doorway.

"Germaine, who was sitting near the fire, turned toward Monica with instinctive wrath. She was about to cry out something vile . . . but the light in Monica's eyes enveloped her and left her dumbfounded. . . . As Monica approached her, Germaine saw that she had a countenance as defenseless as a child's. 'I was just passing by. . . . Would you give me a glass of cider, Germaine?'

"She went to fetch it and rinsed out a glass. Monica drank it. It had been made of rotten apples. Then she said: 'You'd help me a lot, Germaine, if you'd knit some things for me. It isn't a pleasant job, but it would help me a great deal.' She came and sat down in a low chair near her, and looked at her with ineffable tenderness. Suddenly she took her hands in her own: 'Oh, how you have suffered! If you would only look upon me as a friend. . . .' Such force was radiating from Monica that Germaine let her hold on to her hands which were now becoming docile and relaxed. She wanted to answer, but wept instead. Silently, the large tears flowed down her hollow cheeks. She began to sob and cried out: 'This is the first time in two years that I've been able to cry!'

"The mother sighed, for now she was sure her daughter could be saved."

Nothing will soften hardened hearts like humble love. And, besides, there is no more efficacious remedy for timidity. Whether we ourselves are timid, or we find it in others, it is always a barrier that separates people.

People often say that timidity is rooted in pride. At any rate, it always implies an exaggerated self-preoccupation, a fear of being misjudged, of committing a blunder. It is precisely this self-concern that makes it impossible to enter simply and freely into relation with one's equals. When humble love comes and sweeps away all this self-centeredness and self-concern, one feels himself marvelously attuned to his surroundings.

Yet there is something even more painful than our own timidity, and that is the feeling that we frighten others, put them ill at ease, and keep them from being really and truly themselves. The more we cultivate humble love, the more we shall free others from the feeling of inferiority, and the more we shall become accessible to those who approach us.

For humble love will work in us the miraculous transformation so well described by G. Thibon: "Rare indeed are the beings that give us the impression not only of having a soul, but of being only a soul; in them everything loves and nothing judges us; there is no place in them for those eminently social (or anti-social) instincts of self-interest and double-dealing which create a menace to human understanding, and we feel in their presence, in the higher order of spiritual exchange, this sentiment of calm and absolute security that contact with animals, plants, and inanimate things produces." [1]

5. *Beyond Justice*

"It's not just!"

How often we hear this complaint! Sometimes, when it is a question of an injustice suffered by others, indignation can be tinted with a certain nobility. But if it is not followed

[1] *Le Pain de Chaque Jour.*

by a courageous effort to perfect justice, it remains the vainest attitude in the world. Crying over it relieves the one offended, but never produces anything constructive. Besides, the people who usually cry, "It's not just!" consider only the injustice of which they feel they are victims. Since man is full of contradictory desires, he is rarely content with his own lot. "The happiness of this world is made up of so many pieces that it is always missing some of them."

But this is not just an observation of our own day. Hippocrates had already written: "Man is full of folly, void of righteous works, and needlessly suffering from immense toiling. He melts gold and silver, never ceasing to gain it, and always worrying about acquiring more of it . . . some buy dogs, others horses; enclosing a vast area, they call it their own, and they wish to be masters over great domains, while not being masters of themselves. . . . They hasten to marry a wife whom they very soon put aside; they love, then hate. . . . Not having riches, they crave them; once gained, they hoard or waste them. What they seek is what is beyond their fingertips; those on land have an eye for the sea; those on islands long for the mainland. Rulers and kings imagine their subjects happy, while these on the other hand covet royalty. The city's leader envies the tradesman, and the tradesman envies the ruler."

This tendency to complain and to claim one's rights is far from being on the wane in the world today. Although the standard of living has never been so high as in our day and age, at least in some countries, never has there been more discontent. This spirit of asserting one's rights is one of the factors that poisons human relations and, above all, individuals themselves.

Does this mean that there are no injustices in the world?

Is there no war to be waged to eliminate the greatest possible number of them? There is no denying it. But whatever we do, whatever be the excellence of social organization, injustices will keep multiplying, and the social machine itself, while suppressing them, will create new ones. This is why men will be unhappy as long as they do not change their outlook on the world, as long as they will not pass from the *instinct of justice* to the *virtue of justice,* from pagan justice to Christian justice.

In the former, I demand justice from others toward me; in the latter, I busy myself with being just to others, and, to be sure of really accomplishing this, I even go beyond this justice. "You line up at a box-office," writes Dr. Tournier. "You carefully defend your place so as not to lose your turn: this is justice based on equal rights [instinctive justice]. But when you give up your place to an old woman, this is the justice of the Gospel."

Justice in the Gospel is one of the most staggering points of Jesus' message. It is here especially that one sees why Christ came to overthrow the ideas prevalent in His day, and to create in man a new heart, a new soul, a new outlook on the world.

Before His time, justice consisted in behaving toward others just as they behaved toward you, thus rewarding, not only goodness with goodness, but also evil with evil, and violence with violence.

"Christ says: that is not enough. As long as you cling to 'justice,' you will never be guiltless of injustice. As long as you are entangled in wrong and revenge, blow and counter-blow, aggression and defense, you will be constantly drawn into fresh wrong. Passion, by its very definition, surpasses measure. . . .

"If you really want to get anywhere, you must extricate yourself from the whole embroilment and seek a position far removed from all pro's and con's. You must introduce a new force, nor that of self-assertion, but of selflessness; not so-called justice, but creative freedom. Man is really just only when he seeks more than mere justice. More not merely quantitatively, but qualitatively. He must find a power capable of breaking the ban of injustice, something strong enough and big enough to intercept aggression and disarm it: love." [1]

"You have heard that it was said, 'Thou shalt love thy neighbor, and thou shalt hate thy enemy.' But I say to you, love your enemies, do good to those who hate you, and pray for those who persecute and calumniate you, so that you may be children of your Father in heaven, who makes his sun to rise on the good and the evil, and sends rain on the just and the unjust. For if you love those who love you, what reward shall you have? Do not even the publicans do that? And if you salute your brethren only, what are you doing more than others?" (Matt: 5:43–47).

Jesus knows how deceitful the instinct of justice is. Who does not believe himself right when his interests are at stake? It is enough to look ourselves squarely in the face. "It is only a man who is deeply equitable and intelligent that is willing to admit he has not always acted out of a concern for justice."

There is only one way to be just, and that is to be especially concerned for the justice we owe others. It is to go beyond justice in order to let ourselves be guided solely by the will to create good, in all circumstances and with

[1] Romano Guardini, *The Lord,* translated by Elinor Castendyk Briefs (Chicago: Henry Regnery Company, 1954).

regard to all, whatever be their dispositions or attitudes toward us. We must not dream of a world that becomes just, but rather of a world where we ourselves become just.

The day when each one seriously wants it, the world will really become a paradise of justice and love. As the proverb runs: "If each one would sweep in front of his own door, the whole street would be clean."

The day when we, without waiting for others to change, stop complaining and counting the injuries we have received from fate, others, the state, financial affairs, our husband or wife, our contractors, our landlord or tenant—the day when we have but one concern: to throw the weight of our own justice into a world without justice, and do this without wearying of it, then and only then will we take rank among the forces that construct, edify, unite, reconcile, and create. Suddenly we will have found the same peace and joy that we see overflowing in the heart of a St. Francis of Assisi or of a St. Vincent de Paul.

"Admittedly, this is beyond human power. To purify the heart so completely that from the very start respect for the dignity of the other controls the natural passions [for example, the desires of vengeance and reprisals]; to disarm hatred, surrounding it and overcoming its would-be violence in the perfect freedom of love; to return good for evil, benefit for enmity, all this surpasses human strength, and one should not treat such demands lightly." [2]

This is truly participating in the creative goodness of God, resembling the Father whom Jesus Himself shows us as making His sun shine on the good and the evil and His rain fall on the just and the unjust. It is, then, "to participate

[2] Guardini, *op. cit.*

in the sanctity of him whose omnipotence and holiness are contained in the pure freedom of love; hence, of one who stands above good and evil, just and unjust." [3]

It's too much? it's too difficult? Certainly! Yet there is no other solution to the quarrels dividing the world, or to the real injustices men suffer! Would that each one would only force himself every day to become perfect as the Heavenly Father is perfect!

Every solution without this will be lame and will leave men helpless and discontented in a world always on the verge of becoming cut-throat or like a jungle again.

6. *Becoming Interior*

THE love we bear toward our neighbor is a little like the love we have for God. It maintains itself and deepens only through composure, meditation, disinterested attention, and self-renouncement. What most of all menaces our relations with others, even those closest to us, is losing sight of their profound self, their dignity as persons, their eternal destiny, their ties with God—in short, it is losing sight of what always deserves the gift of our heart, and the activity of our creative love. Daily life with its continuous encounters, material necessities, unavoidable differences, and incessant hurts often turns us away from the profound attention that we constantly owe our neighbor. This is the only realistic

[3] *Ibid.*

outlook that tends to coincide with God's point of view. As a result, we no longer see anything but his character, bad habits, manias, limits, tactlessness, and especially the faults *we* have to put up with. We become blind to his visage as brother, friend, or spouse: he risks becoming odious to us or at least far away, estranged, and unwanted.

This is when we should pull ourselves together from the depths of our being, and pray:

"Lord, wake me up! Make me silence all these vicious voices in me: my offended touchiness, my antipathy, hatred, irritation, my vengeance. Pierce me deeply with Your gaze, to make me become more and more transparent, pure, and calm. Help me to deny myself, forget myself, and disappear before my own eyes. Help me to have a peaceful look and to be full of love. And, out of regard for this brother, help me to find again the spontaneity and joy I had on that blessed day when our hearts first met."

Such a prayer, prolonged if need be, brings the heart of Christ into our own. It transforms the regard we have for our neighbor, our brother, friend, or spouse. It helps us overlook his manias, mannerisms, tactlessness, the "accidents" that displease us. It leads us even beyond his talents, qualities, and virtues so as to meet him in the depths of his self, his personality. There we find him in all his unique reality, in his proper destiny, his dramas, his intimate dialogue: his personal debate with the world, with others, with himself, and with God. "He is a man," said St. Francis as he gazed at a youth like himself. "He has to fulfill his tragic destiny. How wonderful! This is an infinite being I behold, a being carrying eternity within him.

Here I have given this man back his just dimension, his ontological value, his sacred reality. And now I have welcomed him anew. Not just in my reason and feelings only, but in my very heart, this deepness within me, now illumined and pacified, is attentive once again, good, tender, a little like God Himself. Now this precious neighbor reposes in my heart as in a peaceful harbor, a fountain of tenderness, and he awakens there all the creative powers God has placed in me for his benefit.

And so my neighbor becomes present and interior to me again. So also do I begin to identify myself with him, to coincide with him, to become him, and thus to love him really as myself.

Julien Green confides to us that he always dreamed of living in personalities other than his own. He imagines a man who, thanks to a magic formula, is able to become those personalities he envies. However, he does not gain in the exchange, and is found in the end miserably dying in his own self again.

We are *ourselves,* and we stay that way. We can only go out of ourselves by entering into others. We become others only through love.

To make our neighbor truly interior to us, there is nothing quite like placing him in our prayer. Let us then plunge him in that which is the best in us: the living and life-giving presence of God.

"When we act in the state of prayer, provided it be true prayer, it is impossible to wrong another."

In fact, with true prayer all is made clear: all grows quiet and takes its just proportions. It is impossible really to approach God without sharing in His thoughts, His point of view, His forbearance, His patience—without participating in His goodness, stability, charity and creative will. When our neighbor contradicts us, offends or irritates us—when he is on the verge of becoming an "object" to us, by placing him in our prayer he reassumes his value as a person.

Remember this too: there are many men we meet in life who ask nothing of us, and many others who do appeal to us and for whom we can do nothing. Every day ends with the sad remembrance of the brothers to whom we could not go—and others, as well, to whom we could not respond because of the limitations of our time, strength, fortune, even our heart.

There is but one force remaining in us then: that of gathering them all in our tenderness, making them intimately present to us, and then placing them in our prayer, confiding them to God's loving omnipotence.

Antoine Martel used to practice this prayerful "interiorization" during his travels. On the way to Cracow in 1930, he noted: "I've been looking at all these strangers with whom I've been riding for hours. They are like beloved brothers whom the Lord put in my path, so that I might help them by my interior prayer, and offer myself at the same time to their fraternity."

Always and everywhere, whether in the street, or some public place, on the streetcar or train, I can thus make the people I meet real to me: the child opening his eyes on life, the old man hobbling along full of infirmities, the man on his way to work, the beggar woman, the couple holding hands, the mother smiling on her child, the fellow with the worried brow, and the one with the mean look. I can put them all in my prayer and offer them to the creative touch of God.

Nothing makes the heart grow bigger. Nothing makes communion with the world more intimate, brings men closer, or makes them more fraternal and real to each other.

7 . *Steadfastness*

How beautiful was our young love!—like a gentle breeze, carrying us toward the open sea. Our skiff cut the waves with joyous and vibrant ease. All our problems seemed resolved; all our questions had their answers; all obstacles had vanished—there was nothing but the immensity of what lay before us, our rapture, our conquest. Softly we echoed the joyous words of the *Imitation*: "Love is an excellent thing, a very great blessing, indeed. It makes every difficulty easy, and bears all wrongs with equanimity. For it bears a burden without being weighted and renders sweet all that is bitter."

But who could speak of bitterness when everything was so perfect? Ours was a way of simplicity, ease, harmony, intimacy, joy, and enchantment—and it seemed it would remain so forever.

But, one day, the appearance of a tiny fault forced itself upon us—a gap hardly perceptible. We thought we were *one;* we were *two.* Oh, it wasn't a question of disagreement; rather it was a tension that was more or less acute. The "other" remained the "other." Close? Yes, so close, but so different!

Then suddenly he behaved in such a way that I could

not agree with him. Momentarily, I lost the luminous path leading to his soul. . . . Then, I found it again.

Soon, however, the discord became more accentuated. Some days I felt as if the one I loved were very distant, as though he had withdrawn into an impenetrable fog. Unforeseen differences of opinion arose over things that were often trivial, but sometimes important. We had our first clash. Even open hostility broke out; we exchanged sharp and cutting words. This was our first argument: it was to be the lowly ancestor of a long line of quarrels of every kind.

So it is that love is proved by fire. Many, alas, do not emerge victorious. Feeling injured or deceived, they cease loving, break their vows, and go their own way. But of what mettle is this kind of love?

Others stay, but live deceived, discouraged, and pledged to a life that is as dull and gloomy as a winter's day.

True love, however, stands firm. It returns to itself and reflects upon itself. It knows that its essential mission is to accept the beloved as he is, and to work daily to make him become what he ought.

Yes, love is no laughing matter.

To love all men in general and to love enemies who are absent is very easy. But to love those who are very close, who continually disturb and upset our peace of mind, without even being aware of it; to put up with their faults without a word, the faults that always irritate us in the same spot, like a perpetual nail in our shoe; to listen to their complaints, their pessimism and despair which veil all the world in black crepe; to be still even when they disturb the recollection we need so badly, and rob us of our time for prayer—so necessary to find our soul in God—this is the inglorious heroism that is daily required of love!

This will perhaps always be love's demand, without any hope of ever seeing the end. If only it were just a question of accepting suffering for a week, a month, or a year! But sometimes we are forced to admit that patience will be required until the last breath, that the real triumph of love will come only by enduring until this last moment.

To forget our own weariness, our disillusionment, and weakness, we must become attentive each day to the miseries of others, listen to their woes, fears, reproaches, and suffering. We must carry these in our own heart, for it is often relief enough for one who suffers just to be able to recite his long litany of troubles to someone. The greatest charity we can show here is to listen in silence, but with all our soul's attention.

Listen! even speak at the right time, but weighing our words well. This too will calm him, rid him of his cares and apprehensions, and ease those anxieties that may leave him today only to return tomorrow.

Of course, there are some who are never satisfied. Though we give them all we can, they accuse us of neglecting and abandoning them. Instead of becoming angry, we must find in ourselves all they need—that last gift; and if they accuse us even then, we must sincerely ask their forgiveness for not being able to do more.

It is probable, even certain, that we will sometimes feel extremely tired of continually carrying someone else's burden. We shall long for a little solitude, to be alone with ourselves, to find a little silence and rest from the world. And if we do get such an opportunity, with God's help, we must make the most of it to find strength and light, to become re-charged with love to enable us to continue along the way. But were it just an escape or an egotistic folding up upon ourselves, the remedy would be far worse than the evil, for in this solitude we would find only our own misery. Coming face to face with one's self in solitude and retreat is vivifying only when we come face to face with God at the same time. He alone is the Love that sustains and renews all love. Nothing is more necessary than to turn to Him frequently and find there the fountain of living water, the well that secretly quenches, with its bottomless source, our human kindness and tenderness—so quick to become dry.

To lose one's soul! Almost all love must pass through this purifying fire. Often one will feel he is being deceived, giving without receiving, losing everything—even himself, and falling into a bottomless pit.

When he comes through the trial victorious, he discovers that, far from losing himself, he has found himself. He has changed. He has taken on a new dimension, a new intensity, a new depth that he could never have dreamed of at the moment of that initial enchantment of his young love.

Besides, he often finds himself closer to God, bathed now in the ocean of His infinite Love. Maxence van der Meersch in *Bodies and Souls* has brought home this truth wonderfully in his hero Michel Doutreval. The value of the novel is perhaps debatable from other points of view, but we cannot help admiring the deeply human philosophy found throughout the whole work. It is a glorification of the love of self-sacrifice.

To love Evelyne and to keep on loving her, "he had had to renounce everything, throw his ambition and pride overboard, together with even the hope of ever being happy, and accept poverty, misery, ugliness, illness, and death." This was real love. He was not daunted by the doubts, discouragements, and trials, nor by the hours of despair when he felt he no longer loved. Here was the miracle in his life, for the day he let his old love die, and no longer demanded or expected anything from Evelyne, the day he devoted himself to her without desiring any return, without scheming or hoping—that very day a new love rose up in him, purified, victorious, and freed from the slavery of egoism. He had given up everything and had been willing to limit his horizon and his life for a poor and wandering creature destined to die, and behold! he found in his own destitution an enthusiasm, splendor, joy, and emotion that the world could never have given him. Here is where he can now seek all his motives for living, all his energy, and his reward.

"Everything has to be earned, whether it is truth, grace, genius, or love itself. And is not the love of man and woman also, like everything else in human life, the symbol and reflection of a great task of love and salvation? For love also demands and promises:

" 'Leave yourself and you shall find me.'

"Michel had had to forget himself, renouncing, shedding his egoism, and literally, as the solemnization of matrimony demands, give himself to death for the other's sake. He had had to expiate. But today, purified of all the material, earthly qualities there had been in him, he loved with a new, indestructible love and could cry out to the woman he loved:

" 'I love you! In spite of all the wretchedness and misery of your humanity, in spite of all your weakness and poverty, and for your weakness' sake and your poverty's sake, for the sake of the renunciation, servitude, suffering, sweat, and tears that you cost me, I love you!' "

And because, when one touches a person's soul, he not only creates his own being but discovers the Being *par ex-*

cellence as well and touches the Infinite, Michel the unbeliever found God.

"The guiding concept of our life seems to be love and self-sacrifice, something inexplicable which craves God.

"Michel did not believe in anything, either. He too denied that life had any meaning or goal. But now, from having loved another human victim for her misery's sake, from having pitied her and been willing to share her tears, hardship, and poverty, now beyond that dear, sad, suffering face another Face shone through. Now behind Evelyne, behind the noble love of sorrowful humanity, there was the love of God."[1]

8. *Love and Liberty*

THERE are three ways of conceiving and living free love. One is detestable. The other two make up the perfection of love.

Usually by free love we understand love that refuses to be bound forever, especially the love uniting man and woman, putting them into the most restricted community of life in the world, the conjugal life. Even here, and especially here, people do not want to hear the word *forever* pronounced. They claim the liberty of releasing themselves

[1] From *Bodies and Souls* by Maxence van der Meersch, translated by Eithne Wilkins. Copyright 1948 by Editions Albin Michel. Used by permission of the publisher, Farrar, Straus and Cudahy, Inc.

from these ties. And they even go so far as to make this freedom one of the foremost qualities of love.

Never has the sense of a word been perverted so naively and so cynically.

Every form of love, especially conjugal love, is the profound adoption of another being in view of creating and promoting it, making it bloom, making it truly itself.

Because the partisans of free love have never conceived of love on this level, they refuse the eternal bonds.

For them there is only sensual and carnal love, pleasure-love, self-love. The person loved does not count. He is never seen as a person, as an object of complete dedication. He is just a tool to be used. And the day I tire of him, the day I can find someone better, especially the day he becomes a burden, I abandon him, reject him as something valueless, to begin *my* life over again, to save *my* happiness, to protect *my* right to love. Me! Me! Always me! And nothing but me!

Nowhere in the world is there such sordid egoism as free love thus conceived.

Listen how cynically Dr. Doutreval expresses it while speaking to his son Michel:

" 'Never let yourself be carried away, Michel. Life wants those with strong minds. Anyone who has achieved great things has always done it, to a greater or lesser degree, by trampling on a certain number of victims. Cromwell, Napoleon. . . . That's what life is like. It's the law of things as they are. Existence is a fight. You won't change it. Take it as it is. Don't be simple-minded; don't stuff yourself up with empty dreams. Be strong. Try to know, young as you are, what men usually discover as a result of hard experience: that love doesn't count. It passes. One falls in love ten times, or twenty. You'll see. You will love heaven knows how many women in your life . . . and every time you'll mean it! And every time you'll console yourself for love, no matter how tremendous it may be.

" 'So act accordingly. I don't forbid you to amuse yourself and get some fun out of life. Fall in love if you like. But keep your head. Keep a critical eye on yourself in love; recognize that it's a mere fit of madness, without being ashamed of it, of course, for everyone goes through it. But distinguish yourself from other men who believe in it, by not believing in it yourself; and don't let it sweep you off your feet and perhaps over a precipice. Believe me, one can very easily make love and common sense come to terms with each other. One can do all sorts of absurd things so long as one only reserves the future, never taking love seriously and knowing the moment the delirium must stop. The main thing is to stop in time. Have you understood me?'

" 'I think so,' Michel murmured.

" 'You may say to me: so that involves there being a victim every time? Well, yes. It's sad; it's deplorable; but that's how it is. Life demands it. Life feeds on death. That's why I tell you to be strong. You are a member of an elite. You have the right to go far. You will have a brilliant scientific career. I'm preparing you for it. You will inherit my work, defending it and continuing it. You will render humanity the most priceless services. That deserves victims. You won't succeed at all if you call a halt before the first insignificant creature and don't dare to pass on. In this world, Michel, there are plenty of people who are there simply to serve the progress of the elite. That's the only explanation of things possible. So make up your mind and be a man. No woman can be anything more than a tool for you—or a pastime'."[1]

To understand love thus is to push self-love to the absolute despising of others.

However, there is a liberty we ought to acquire toward those we love, a very special kind of liberty, difficult and even impossible to understand as long as we have not experienced it deep within ourselves.

It is usually called "detachment."

Most of us recoil as soon as we hear the word. We do not see how it is possible for love and detachment, love and liberty, to be united. It is either one or the other.

And yet. . . .

Christ has asked us to love our brothers and our neighbors, and at the same time, not to love them more than Him, lest we be unworthy of Him. Here is the whole mystery.

We must love our parents, our friends, our brothers, and everyone in the world, but in their rank as creatures, never as gods. My heart may fix itself upon no one as an absolute, reposing there as in my final end. To nothing, to no one may we say: you are my all; you are my life; you are the all of my life.

Our heart usually tends to divinize the object of its love: a father or mother, husband or wife, a child, even a home. So, with respect to all we must stay free. We must be ready to lose them temporally, bodily (not necessarily without a wound: Jesus Himself wept over His friend Lazarus), but without murmuring, without revolt. Haven't we told God that we love Him "above all things"? The moment the dearest thing in the world is torn away from us, then we

[1] Maxence van der Meersch, *Bodies and Souls.*

can prove the sincerity of our words, and see if God really is our all, if our heart is really a free heart.

Detachment by no means signifies indifference.

"*Indifference* means, 'You absolutely do not exist for me.'

"*Attachment* means, 'You exist, but your existence hinges on our reciprocal relations. You exist insofar as I possess you.'

"*Detachment* signifies, 'You exist for me, absolutely, even outside our personal relations, above and beyond all you can give me; I adore in you a reflection of the divinity from which nothing can snatch me; and I need not possess you in order that you exist for me.' "[2]

Detachment is the sign *par excellence* of the purity of love. One who loves with detachment and liberty knows that he is entrusting the object of his tenderness to One more loving and powerful than he himself. His only wish is to be a cause of each one's growth, development, and happiness—a cause that has been delegated by the First Cause to work toward making men become what they ought.

Suppose this Cause withdraws its delegation from us, or changes its mode: our love can do no more than supply for and give over every place to God's love. Why shouldn't we say with deep humility and even a touch of joy: "You gave them to me; You have taken them away. Blessed be Your Holy Name!"

One who thus keeps his heart free is perhaps the only one who can in turn create free hearts—following God's example! For God treats us with an infinite respect because of the liberty He has given us. He wants from us only free allegiance, and not the groveling of slaves. Even when we

[2] G. Thibon, *Le Pain de Chaque Jour.*

have abused our liberty in estranging ourselves from Him, He pursues us with His love. He does not force us. Our gift is to be a heart that is sovereignly free. Here, without a doubt, is love's supreme perfection.

But, unfortunately, most men conceive of love only on the level of the egotistical instinct. For them, to love is to possess, to have for oneself, to dominate, invade, burden, and enslave.

They do not seem to have the slightest notion of a love that helps another being to become free, that freely gives itself for the good of another.

Who knows how much ravage is worked in this world by possessive love? Dr. Paul Tournier paints a somber picture of it in one of his books. The possessive love of parents is especially grave. It would be well if all parents would meditate on these pages. Here the author is describing the cases of psychological troubles brought on by a mother's possessive love.

"There are some whose mothers have kept them away from life and society, out of a concern to protect them from the dangers of the world. Certain parents are very quick to become jealous of every other person, teachers or parents, capable of influencing their child. Some people have been thwarted in their tastes, and in their vocation, because their parents had their own ambitions to fulfil.

"Take the mother who wants her daughter to study because she always regretted the fact that she never had the opportunity herself. She forbids her to go to the ball, not because she is against dancing, but for fear that it will hurt her studies: she might dream more about social life than the intellectual life.

"Then there is the young woman, already adult, who

has never been able to receive a letter without her mother's reading it.

"Here is a woman already engaged a year without ever being able to see her fiancé outside her mother's presence.

"Look at this mother whose love for her son has been so possessive that she has been sick ever since his marriage. In such a situation the daughter-in-law ought to take drastic measures to tear the lad out of his mother's grasp.

"Here we touch upon the drama of domineering love: by wanting to keep the loved one in our possession, we lose him; for this kind of love crushes. Then, either the crushed child vegetates, folds up in himself and falls into neurosis, to the despair of his mother, or he revolts to her great consternation—such inconceivable ingratitude!

"A mother once came to me to make an appointment for her son—a man in his forties! To her amazement, I told her that since her son was of age, he could make his own appointment, if he wanted one. His confidence was aroused by the incident, and soon he came to see me; then I surveyed the disaster. His mother had suffered bitterly from the divorce of her own parents, and so she had entered into life with a 'need' of revenge. First of all, she had exercised it on her husband until the day he left her, then on her son, whom she dominated like a despot, finally upon the one who should have been her daughter-in-law, but whom she chased away—not to mention a daughter of her own who fell sick from it all. From this state of affairs the son had found no escape other than drink—a reason for his mother to dominate him all the more—to *save* him."[3]

The maternal instinct is certainly a tremendous force, but terrible dangers lie hidden within. "A mother can throw

[3] Paul Tournier, *De la solitude à la Communauté.*

herself in front of a train to save her child, and be unable all the while to give up certain plans she had made for his future, to the detriment of the child's happiness."[4]

Here, the author is quite exact in his description of the drama of maternal love. Will it be only an instinct, a purely biological drive, with spurts of devotion now and then, along with unconscious tyrannical egoisms as well?—or will it become a truly human love that is spiritual, purified from self-interest, and solely concerned with engendering a being that is more and more free?

The author adds: "This instinct should help the mother reach a conscious and serious renunciation of self. As long as it does not attain this, it remains pure instinct."[5]

This increasing purification means a hard trial for mothers all their life. In this child who is flesh of their flesh, they must one day produce a person that is free, autonomous, self-disposed, able to act by himself, engaged in a destiny that must be realized with more and more total independence.

True maternal love victoriously goes through all these crises staked out as landmarks in a mother's life, and is directed toward a self-denial that is more and more complete.

This renunciation begins in the child's infancy where there is a strong temptation to spoil him, to stop his crying, to win his caresses.

The second crisis occurs when the child approaches adolescence and truly faces life. These are baffling years for parents. The child begins to love outside the family circle. He is not satisfied with his own family. He needs comrades,

[4] Etienne de Greeff, *Notre destinée et nos instincts.*
[5] *Ibid.*

friends of his own age. His personality asserts itself in opposition to his parents. He has ideas of his own, and he affirms his wishes more and more. This is the moment when the eaglet spreads his wings and wants to try his luck at free flight. This is a critical moment for parents. They ought to redouble their efforts to understand him and to respect his unfolding personality, and let him go ahead with his first experiments, under their discreet control.

The danger is great for the mother (and the father too) to look upon her grown boy or girl as still a little child for whom every event must be looked out for and decided. Her intervention, though it be very tender, will almost always make the victim groan inside, or incite open revolt or contention. "How ungrateful," she will think to herself; "it's only for his own good." In fact, it is his good that she wishes, but she wishes it badly, letting herself be influenced too much by her own personality instead of caring solely for her child.

"Many of these domineering parents," writes Dr. Tournier, "send me their child at the moment when he begins to escape them and turns to manifestations of independence which they consider outrageous or dangerous. They are always convinced that they are motivated only by concern for their child's well-being. They want to make a weapon out of me to win the battle between their will and that of their self-asserting child. They expect that surely a Christian doctor will not fail to preach submission to their authority. Furthermore, they are dumbfounded and abashed when I seek rather to understand their child, and to help him become conscious of his personal aspirations which had been suppressed for so long."

However, the most critical moment without a doubt comes when the child chooses a state in life: a religious vocation or marriage.

There are admirable mothers who, from the moment they knew a child was going to be given to them, have offered this son or daughter to God's exclusive service, if it be His will. Should the Lord call him, they give him up generously, and by their prayers they help him to respond fully to his vocation.

There are others, unfortunately, who become frightened at the thought of the renunciation, the risks, the spiritual adventure, that the future priest or religious takes upon himself in such a life. Then, under the pretext of saving their "little one" from his "thoughtless" enthusiasm, they undertake a "cold war" that gradually stifles the ideals of the young man or woman.

There is the same danger present when it is a question of marriage. Of course we ought to advise parents to enlighten their children concerning the future, counsel them against the caprice of emotions, lead them to a choice where all elements are harmonized as perfectly as possible: religion, family, social, and even economic position.

But the essential condition remains, nonetheless, harmony between persons; and when two hearts are pledged to one another, there is no need to pronounce a veto except for really grave reasons. How often it is that parents show a blind hostility or an attitude that reveals distaste for the slightest social differences—"you could have done better"— or simply because the fiancé does not please them. Imagining that they are assuring the good of their child, they take his place in an essential choice, often just following the impulses of their vanity, pride, or irritability.

Finally, there is a great temptation to intrude upon the home-life of a son or daughter under the pretext of giving them good advice. A lawyer once told me that eighty per cent of the divorces have as their basic cause the abusive or clumsy intervention of parents in their children's household. At a time like this, more than ever, one must step out of the picture, be quiet, and give advice only if asked; moreover, one must accept the disappointment if they do not follow it.

Parents should be reassured that the more their children sense their liberty respected, the more they will stay attached to them and hold them in profound veneration.

And this is true of all forms of love: especially of friendship and married love.

"By wanting to keep the loved one in our possession, we lose him." By loving him with a liberating love, we attach ourself to him forever.

9. Respect

"WE WOULD like men to respect us, Sire."

When a Belgian miner said this to King Albert, he expressed one of man's deepest aspirations. This man had more need of respect than of bread. If at times he vehemently demands bread, it is not solely to appease his hunger —for in the thoughtful provision of his daily bread, man sees one of the principal signs of respect that can be afforded to his person.

We cannot help noticing this: every man instinctively

carries within him the feeling of his importance, of his value and dignity.

It is very natural for him to over-evaluate secondary things: intelligence, knowledge, talent, power, richness, success, physical beauty, and position. He easily gives way to pretension, to pompousness, and pride. . . . There is in most of us a naive vanity which dies, they say, about a quarter of an hour after our last breath.

But every man in his marginal and semi-obscure consciousness has the impression that he is a unique case, a focal point, a creature who never can be reduced simply to the role of a tool, a being infinitely precious, upon which others ought to look differently than they look upon the rest of the world.

Such a man is perfectly right. In his and God's mind, he is a being endowed with a unique greatness. Each of us has a spiritual soul, conscious of itself, free, immortal, destined to intimate relations with God, now and throughout all eternity. In a way we are all constituted as absolutes in the face of other men and in the face of God Himself.

It is very desirable, then, that man become more and more aware of his dignity as a human person. When this consciousness diminishes in him, when, by all sorts of vexations, someone has succeeded in stripping him of it almost completely, he often ceases to be a man; he is ripe for every despair and crime, and passes onto the level of the blind forces of nature.

In a singular way, by giving consideration to our neighbor that is penetrated with respect (whatever station, intelligence, or virtue he may have), we help him become conscious of this primary dignity.

"We must treat all the tools of the monastery as sacred objects," says Saint Benedict.

All the more, then, man!

Respect is truly the soul of love and charity.

Nothing moves a man more than to see himself considered in his ontological value, in the realness of his person, in his soul.

In the story of his conversion, René Leyvraz recounts how, at the moment he was about to take the decisive step, he went to a convent of French religious at Constantinople, where he was living at the time. He knew no one there, and had written a note to explain the motive for his visit. Upon entering the parlor, the religious who had read the letter murmured in a low voice: "A soul."

"That soul trembled in me with anxious expectation," writes the convert. "Who, up till then, had shown concern for it? Who had pitied it and its abandonment? . . . At that moment, I felt the value of a soul for the Church, and the immense solicitude with which it gathers in souls. Can anyone understand this in a world that is so carnal, and seeped in materialism? My soul was at stake. They could have spoken to me, without touching me, of earthly happiness, of fortune, glory, and art. But my soul was at stake and I felt overwhelmed."

If only people would understand this! When we speak of respect, we are not just concerned with that merely exterior and simply negative attitude that consists in avoiding all cutting words or ill-willed actions toward our neighbor. We are rather concerned with that positive and active respect that really gives our neighbor the impression of being someone precious and sacred.

This respect should accompany all forms of love, especially the most intimate ones. The more bodies and souls come into contact, and the more intimate the communion between beings becomes, so much the more should they envelop one another in respect. This does not harm their familiarity or intimacy. On the contrary, it gives man a quality that is indefinable, a flavor that is exquisite. All vulgarity is a false note that separates souls and is a menace to love.

Nor should we exclude anyone from this respect. It is not addressed primarily to qualities or talents, nor to anything accidental in man, but to his very being: "If someone loves me for my good judgment, or for my memory, does he really love me? No, for I can lose these qualities without losing myself." Thus wrote Pascal. We could say as well: "If someone respects me for my wealth, my power, or the place I occupy, does he really respect me?" No, for I can lose all these without losing myself. "All love that has as its formal basis something other than the intermingling of my self with another's in a reciprocal communion is an illusion."[1]

Without a doubt it is not necessary, the first time we meet someone, to experience the joyous tremor we feel when we meet our family or our friends. But no man should ever come in contact with us, even briefly, and go away wounded with the feeling that he has been only a thing to us, and not a man.

Simone Weil, in *Waiting for God,* very rightly says that attention is the essential of prayer. But she continues: "Not only does the love of God have attention for its substance; the love of our neighbor, which we know to be the same

[1] Maurice Nédoncelle, *La réciprocité des consciences.*

love, is made of this same substance. Those who are unhappy have no need for anything in this world but people capable of giving them their attention. The capacity to give one's attention to a sufferer is a very rare and difficult thing; it is almost a miracle; it *is* a miracle. Nearly all those who think they have this capacity do not possess it. Warmth of heart, impulsiveness, pity are not enough. . . .

"The love of our neighbor in all its fullness simply means being able to say to him: 'What are you going through?' It is a recognition that the sufferer exists, not only as an item in a collection, or a specimen from the social category labeled 'unfortunate,' but as a man, exactly as we are, who was one day stamped with a special mark of affliction. For this reason it is enough, but it is indispensable, to know how to look at him in a certain way.

"This way of looking is first of all attentive. The soul empties itself of all its own contents in order to receive into itself the being it is looking at, just as he is, in all his truth."[2]

In no circumstance may we lay aside this respect for man, not even for the vilest Judas, the cruelest tyrant, or the most wretched criminal.

This does not mean that we must stop combatting or punishing them. A person must know how to wage war when he is forced into it, and he must see to it that justice is done. True as this may be, we ought to battle with a spirit sovereignly free of all sentiments of vengeance or hatred. "Joan of Arc did not hate the English: she limited herself to putting them in their place—in the very literal sense of the word: outside of France."[3]

[2] Simone Weil, *Waiting for God,* translated by Emma Crawford (New York: G. P. Putnam's Sons, 1951).

[3] Gustave Thibon, *Retour au réel* (Lyon: Lardanchet, 1943).

We should exercise justice with a deep and sincere sadness at having to reestablish order and right by such severe means. The most fallen of men remains a creature of God, preserves his divine vocation, and retains his title as a soul redeemed by the blood of Christ. This dignity remains indestructible.

Can love have a more beautiful mission than to recreate in man faith in his eternal value? What must have been the emotion of Zacheus, the publican, when he saw Christ stop and call to him: "Zacheus, hurry down, for I must spend today with you"? Greater still must have been the surprise of the adulteress, after the Pharisees had gone, when she heard these liberating words fall from Jesus' lips: "Has no one condemned thee? Nor shall I the more condemn thee. Go, and sin no more."

The first belonged to a profession where one was almost infallibly taken for a thief; the second felt herself surrounded by hatred, and yielded beneath the shame. And behold! someone spoke to them with respect. They felt loved in spite of their sins. Yes, the Master, of whom everyone spoke, believed in them and stirred up hope in them, the desire for a righteous life.

"If one day the wicked have an excuse," writes Lavelle, "they will only be able to find this: that no one loved them."

"Oscar Wilde," writes Zundel, "in the abyss of disgrace, and involved in a scandalous lawsuit that exposed his private life to the eyes of all England, owed his salvation solely to the profound reverence shown to him by a single friend, who stayed faithful to him, and whose respect at that time appeared to him as a promise of redemption. There was someone who paid homage to something that public disgrace had not touched, and this encouragement gave him freedom. This gesture enlightened his captivity, this advance of love allowed him to rediscover that great Love, to such an extent as to compel him to write that the most precious day of his life was the day society sent him to prison."

10. *Called to Attention*

WE have seen how Simone Weil puts the essence of love of neighbor in *attention*. Again she says: "Love for our neighbor, being made up of creative attention, is analogous to genius." Because this is such an important idea, let us reflect upon it a bit more.

Did you ever find yourself in a large group? Conversation was at its height, but you were alone . . . in your corner. People passed without noticing you. No one paid you the slightest attention. You felt as if you didn't exist. Suddenly, someone came and drew you out of your solitude, and you experienced the joyous feeling of existing again.

This experience ought to cure us of ever being inattentive to those with whom we come into contact.

Attention is one of the principal manifestations of the respect and charity we owe our neighbor. It is like a profound prayer to Him. To pay attention to someone is to judge him worthy of our soul's consideration, though it be but for an instant. By attention we enter into communion with our neighbor and make him proud to exist. We feel ourselves respected as a man when someone looks upon us with attention.

Perhaps we could save men from ruin if we were more attentive. Here is a striking example of this truth: Evelyn, the daughter of Professor Lubert, decided to kill herself, since the unhappiness her suicide will cause seems to be the only way to tear her father away from the woman who had given poison to her mother to get her out of the way.

Instinctively, however, before putting her plan into operation, Evelyn went to different people to find the help that might save her. But no one saw the death she bore in her eyes. When someone asked an old friend of the family, Professor Courtelain, about her, he noted that she had been a little sad and out of sorts, but his observation was a little too late.

One of her friends, a young man-about-town, had even joked when she said to him sadly: "To think I came to you for help!"

The old pastor, in a hurry to get back to his poor flock, left her just when she was about to confide in him. Only later did he "realize" that he had been dealing with a soul in despair.

The man who offered her the orangeade did not "notice" the distress in her eyes and gestures. He did not voice that word of friendship that could have alleviated her profound and justified sorrow.

Each one will have his share of responsibility for her death.

"Our life," said the pastor, "can hang on a single moment of tenderness and pity, and I did not make this gesture. You can easily see how I am to blame."

"So are we all," added Professor Courtelain. "She placed her friendship in me. She came to me and I took her distress lightly, Father—that same distress she later brought to you. We are all guilty of inattention in life."[1]

Attention has a liturgy all its own.

It is not enough that it exist in the heart and soul. It should manifest and express itself in signs: a look, a word, a smile, a gesture.

One of the most important ways of showing our attention toward others is to greet them, to say "hello."

In villages everyone greets one another. And it is great praise when someone can say of you: "He has such a friendly greeting," or again, "He gave me such a cheerful 'hello.' "

On the other hand, not to say "good day," not to answer a greeting is a sign of vanity, of disgust, grouchiness, or hate. "They no longer say 'hello.' "

Nothing is more winning than a greeting, especially when a smile goes with it. I knew a young girl who died in the full bloom of her youth and who left many vivid regrets behind her; among these was the regret of an old workman who used to pass through her neighborhood on his way to work each morning. The greeting she gave him was so radiant and fresh that his whole day was brightened by it. She could have passed him by without saying anything, but it would have meant a little less joy in the old man's heart.

All of us at sometime have to enter a hotel, a hospital, or a factory. Don't pass by the doorman as if he were a dog in a kennel! Even if you have no need of his services, give him a little sign of friendship and say "good day" to him with a smile. If you have thoughtlessly forgotten him, turn around, go back, and greet him. He is a man just like you and he

[1] Henri Bordeaux, *L'Intruse*.

needs this. It will warm his heart. He will thank you more for that than for your tip.

If you are an employer, director, engineer, or foreman— if, in short, you are a superior or manager anywhere, don't forget to say "good morning." And be the *first* to say it! If it is possible, give each person your particular attention for a moment. This greeting tears people away from anonymity. It gives each one the feeling that he really exists for you, that he is not just another cog in the machine, but a real person with a soul of his own.

I once saw a delightful scene at a gymnastic meet. Among the thousands who were performing were two hundred young girls from the Dutch province of Limbourg. Their bishop was assisting at the demonstration and more than once they filed by the rostrum where he presided among other dignitaries. Each time their smiles met with such warmth that each child appeared as if she personally knew him. It was truly the Good Shepherd who knew his flock and whose flock knew him.

The power of a greeting! Especially when we can add a name to it!

Dale Carnegie writes that "a man's name is to him the sweetest and most important sound in the English language."

There is a mysterious identification between a person and the name he bears. The name evokes the person in his totality and in his profound self. We call someone dear when we pronounce his name. We make him present to us. For this reason the name demands the same respect as the person.

When someone has forgotten our name, we feel as if we

were forgotten; when someone murders it by pronouncing it badly or by misspelling it, even without notice, it is as if he had not deemed us worthy of his interest. We feel slightly irritated by it, especially if it happens repeatedly.

What, then, is to be said for the mania to intentionally deform names or to dub others with nicknames? Most of the time this mania reveals a desire to slight or humiliate our neighbor. There is no doubt that nicknames are usually the weapons of weak people who take base revenge upon their superiors by this means. In every instance, it is a sign of vulgarity. The more one descends the social scale, the more the nickname is used. In the world of thieves and robbers, one is designated by a nickname only.

How pitiable, moreover, are those who find themselves deprived of their names—who are just a number in a hospital!

A young worker once said: "The other day I went to see one of my companions in one of the wards. Although he had been in this same ward for at least three months, I was amazed to find him still called by a number. I know well enough that the nurses can't remember the names of all the newcomers, but when a person has been there over a long period, there is no excuse. A number is anonymous. It has no personality. The person is nothing but a puppet or a machine which they nurse to make it run better—which they repair so it can function again. We are not numbers, but human beings."

The memory for names confers an extraordinary prestige on a group leader, a business man, a man in politics, or the head of an enterprise.

Napoleon I aroused the enthusiasm of his soldiers and

obtained the greatest sacrifices from them thanks to his skill in remembering the name of those whom he wanted to congratulate for some brilliant action. He thus created the legend that he personally knew each one of the innumerable fighting men in his army.

As to Napoleon III, "he boasted that in spite of all his royal duties he could remember the name of every person he met. His technique? Simple. If he didn't hear the name distinctly, he said, 'So sorry, I didn't get the name clearly.' Then, if it was an unusual name, he would say, 'How is it spelled?' During the conversation, he took the trouble to repeat the name several times, and tried to associate it in his mind with the man's features, expression, and general appearance.

"If the man were someone of importance, Napoleon went to even further pains. As soon as His Royal Highness was alone, he wrote the man's name down on a piece of paper, looked at it, concentrated on it, fixed it securely in his mind, and then tore up the paper. In this way, he gained an eye impression of the name as well as an ear impression."[2]

Another way to show our respect and our attention is by the tone of our voice!

Nothing reveals a man's capital fault more than the habitual tone of his voice.

There is the *bored* tone: "What! Are you still there!"
The *indifferent* tone: "What does that matter to me?"
The *impatient* tone: "What else do you want?"
The *insolent* tone: "Don't think that I'm afraid of you!"
The *grumbling* tone: "You did everything wrong again!"

[2] Dale Carnegie, *How to Win Friends and Influence People* (New York: Simon & Schuster, 1936).

The *scoffing* tone: "But, my dear, can anyone be so naive?"

The *mocking* tone: "And you think it *really* happened?"

The *suspicious* tone: "But you know, people just don't do that to me."

The *irritated* tone: "The world has it in for me, and I have it in for the world."

Don't all of these tones reveal a certain disrespect in speaking to a child of God?

The most troubling thing is that we do not hear ourselves as others hear us.

When someone knocks at our door and we answer "Come in," is it always a welcoming and engaging tone, or is it the impatient tone of a man who is disturbed in the midst of his occupations?

When we pick up the receiver and say "Hello," does it mean "You are welcome, sir," or is it, as our hearer must interpret it, "Oh, what a bore! You always call at the wrong time!"

When we give an order to someone under us, is it with grace, simplicity, and politeness, or is it sour, as if we anticipated some resistance and wished to prevent it?

When we refuse a service that is asked, is it with such a sincere regret, and done in such a charming way that the visitor goes away as content as if he had gained his request; or is it in a way so peevish that he leaves, discontented and put out?

When we make a remark, is it in a benevolent and encouraging tone, or in an irritated and aggressive one?

Who is going to tell us?

If only someone would record our voice, especially at

certain moments, without our knowing it! Our surprise would doubtlessly be like that of the young man at a party who had monopolized the conversation all evening.

"Did I really speak to you *that* way," he said to a comrade. "Please forgive me."

Other than recordings, we only have those who live with us. But most of the time they are afraid to tell us, and, besides, would we believe them?

11. *The Power of a Smile*

THE Chinese have a delightful proverb: "The man who doesn't know how to smile ought not to go into business.

"A smile costs nothing, but it gains much.

"It lasts but an instant, but the memory of it often lasts a lifetime.

"One cannot buy, beg, borrow, or steal it.

"But it is worth absolutely nothing unless it is given.

"So, when you meet someone too tired to give you a smile, give him yours.

"For no one has more need of a smile than he who has none to offer."

*　　*　　*

The smile is one of the most marvelous gifts God has given to man. More than the laugh, it is one of the signs of man's spiritual soul, one of the manifestations of his inner life, one of the revelations of his secret self.

The laugh is more superficial. Although in many cases it is a healthy relaxation, and therefore legitimate and beneficial, it manifests only common and banal reactions, and not what lies deep down in the soul. The smile, on the other hand, shows the depths of a being on its lips and in its eyes. We laugh among comrades. We smile among friends and loved ones.

Claudel wrote that it is the *animus* that laughs in us, whereas it is the *anima* that smiles in us; and it is the smile that is one of the best means of expressing this silent and wondrous thing.

I know there are many kinds of smiles: the puzzling smile by which one conceals his soul rather than gives it; the sceptical smile by which one advertises his defiance toward others, his inner boredom, or his absolute aloofness from everything; the scornful smile by which one thinks he is affirming his superiority over others; the mocking smile by which one puts himself on guard against or challenges an adversary. This list could go on and on.

But these are corruptions of the smile. The smile can only reveal our profound self; and when this profound self is troubled, how can the smile help but reflect it?

"When in doubt whether a stranger is dangerous or not, just look at his smile; his smile will be an indication, if not positive proof."[1]

The smile was originally granted us so that we could offer our neighbor our profound self and gladden him by the communion our soul would then have with his own.

Look at little children. When they do not smile, their mothers feel they only half possess them. Each day the mother watches for the appearance of this sign of the

[1] Henri de Montherlant, *La reine morte* (Paris: Librairie Gallimard, 1947).

spiritual soul's presence in the tiny body; she coaxes it, and when it finally blooms on the tiny lips, she rejoices over it: the tiny soul has just revealed itself; it has just created its first truly human relations—person to person, it has just given itself and restored to the mother the joy of living it owes to her.

In one of her novels, Lucie Delarue-Mardrus shows a young girl of fourteen, the daughter of an alcoholic, who, as a result, has grown up without guidance or love. Her mother died while giving birth to a little sister, for whom the girl is unable to care. The baby is finally given to a nurse, but her sister finds out that she is being badly cared for, and more out of pride than out of sisterly affection, she takes back the child and brings her home. But it isn't long before she notices what a very heavy burden she has taken on, and after some time she decides to entrust her to a more skilfull nurse, so that she can be free to chase through the woods with her dog.

But as she is about to carry out this plan, a wonderful thing happens. The baby sister smiles at her for the first time, and by this she seems to say: "It's me . . . and that's you, and we know each other . . . we are not strangers to each other . . . we understand each other."

At once the girl takes heart. She will no longer leave the little one; she will give up her own pleasure to care for her.

The smile of a little child is a true gift of the soul! This is the only kind of smile he knows, because he is so young: fresh, open, simple, without self-love, and without resentment; his smile is, together "with music and prayer, one of those great gateways to the mystery, not of darkness, but of light."

Later, when life has filled the soul with cares and troubles, when one has clashed with the misunderstandings of some and the ill-will of others, the smile becomes very difficult at times. It passes to the level of an ascetic exercise. In certain lives or at certain times it can demand real heroism. The smile, then, is a great victory over the forces that tend to close up our souls.

There are some men, alas, who no longer have the strength to give a little of their soul in a smile. They continually present a stony face in which no flame glows. Was it not said of a great financier that he always had the air of a man following his own hearse? But he gave generously to the poor and to certain projects. It's a great thing to give a thousand dollars. But in giving it with a smile, you double the amount.

* * *

The winning power of a smile! Rare are the men who can resist it. A young priest who was laboring among the workers in the "Red" zone of Paris said to Julien Green, "They swear at us sometimes, but they have never come to blows. What is necessary is to smile when things go badly. A smile almost always puts things in order."

And the power of a smile makes men grow and develop. It is said of a gruff man that, when he smiles, he makes himself human. A smile is like a sunrise on the face of man, brightening all his surroundings. What a change there would be in homes, communities, and factories if the people there were preoccupied with smiling! Home would be a paradise if father and son, tired as they may be, would have the courage to come home from work with a smile, and if mother, in spite of her fatigue, would also welcome them with a smile, and renew her efforts to do the same each day.

A smile! Charity costing nothing save the will to keep my soul open to all, ready to welcome all!

12. *Loving Begets Understanding*

"An intelligent man is one who understands what I say."

Thus spoke a twelve-year-old boy.

A child's words, yet how profound! A great deal of finesse is required in the art of understanding the soul of another, especially when it is unaware of itself and expresses itself clumsily. Perhaps it would be more exact to say that a charitable man is one who understands his fellow men.

But we must be more exact, since there are two ways of understanding others.

There are narrow-minded psychologists and psychiatrists who are satiated with knowledge; there are soulless dilettantes who make subtle analyses of others, but who never penetrate into the mystery of another's personality.

They consider men as *objects* of study, not as subjects for consideration and love. They do not really put themselves in another's place; they in no way become interior to them, nor do they communicate or become one with them. They lack the gift of sympathy.

Because of this, they miss many things in spite of the perfection of their science and techinques. We do not deny that these things are precious, but in man (just as in the universe, in God, and the Christian mystery) there are depths which reveal themselves only to love.

To be understood! This is already the befuddled aspiration of the child who cries because someone has scolded him, when he believed he had accomplished a great feat or made a great discovery.

Here is how one woman recalls such a tragedy. It happened when she was four years old.

"My sisters, who attended boarding school during the day, were not home. Alone in the garden, not too far from the house, I happened to pick up a little branch from a tree —somehow the bark obediently slid off in my hands. Surprised, I continued to peel off the bark, and, lo and behold, from the fallen-away bark emerged a smooth, white stick of ivory.

"An indescribable wonder seized me. Breathless with joy I ran to the house, and rushed into the room where my mother and Miss Corner were sitting. I could hardly speak:

" 'It's *me* who did it!'

"They didn't even lift their heads. The Englishwoman, with her usual tone, corrected my faulty phrase:

" 'It is *I* who have done it,' she said.

". . . Not a word.

"Then, her tone lost all patience:

" 'Do you mean to say: "*I* did it?" '

"My head fell dizzily. I kept my silence.

" 'Is *that* what you mean to say?' . . .

"The incomprehensible stubbornness of children! Shaken by the arm, I shriveled up in my silence. Soon Mama and the Englishwoman rose. The little, miraculous branch hung in my trembling hand. It had lost all its enchantment.

"That was the only time my mother ever scolded me."

The desire to be understood becomes even more intense during adolescence. This is the age when one discovers life, the universe, beauty, enthusiasm, love, and melancholy in the secret garden of his soul, and when he fears to appear ridiculous in the eyes of a world that seems to take so little interest in these values that money can neither buy nor measure. It is the age of problems, of interior tensions, of troubles of conscience, of "faults" for which, thank God, we are not to blame. And we would so like to meet someone who would welcome our confidence, without judging us, yet with a deep understanding and an encouraging sympathy.

We need a big heart to understand some people—especially those who have suffered, those whose mourning, failure, financial set-back, accident, sickness, disgrace, or abandonment have marked their existence with the seal of "unhappiness."

How difficult it is to realize exactly their state of soul, if we have not known in our own flesh or in our own heart trials just as bitter.

The great danger at such times is to pass near them hastily, indifferently, thoughtlessly, offering them mere pious platitudes in conventional formulas, sometimes even with futile jokes under the pretext of cheering them up. All this leaves them more lonely than before. It just increases their sorrow. They feel that we have not understood anything, that we cannot enter into their drama . . . that we just do not understand the situation.

It is true that we do not ever know it as they do, and it is simpler, humbler, and without a doubt more comforting to those suffering, to confess our ignorance, trying to overcome it all the while. We lack the lived experience of many sufferings. It is not enough to know that there is sadness in the world. We ought to have been through it, endured it, and suffered it ourselves. We should have at least studied and gazed long and deep at it with our soul.

"You know that many children die, but it has never bothered you, because you have never seen a mother before her baby's lifeless body.

"You know that disease is rampant in the country, but this has never bothered you, because you have never seen the struggle of a tubercular clinging to life, and dying at the age of twenty-five.

"You know that there are slums, but this has never bothered you, because you have never seen what it is to go to bed every night nine in a room.

"You know that there are orphans, but this has never bothered you, because you never walked behind a coffin with a seven-year-old boy alone in the world.

"It is not your fault, you don't know—your intellect knows, you have seen it and heard it: sometimes it even seemed to you that it was harped on a little too much, but your heart and your soul do not know it."

Suffering causes revolts; and during a visit nothing is more saddening than to receive words that overflow with bitterness, gall, and recrimination against everything, against everyone, against God. Above all, then, we must give our soul's undivided attention without saying a word, for we can only aid those in distress by listening to them. Perhaps the day will come when we will be able to turn them away gently from their self-absorption, and direct their attention again to others, their fellow sufferers. They also have a mission of goodness to fulfill in the world, and their unhappiness even makes them more apt to fraternize, to understand, and to help. When they have found the way to their neighbor again, it is very likely that they will also rediscover the way to God, and will love Him with an even greater love.

Suffering also makes saints. Sickness, for instance, is

sometimes the occasion of an elevating experience that is both human and spiritual. Cut off from the world and refined by hardship, certain sick people discover true values they had not known previously or had known only superficially. They reach a new level, and a higher world, unknown to most of those in good health.

These people are the most difficult to understand, and we ought to be very humble before them.

France Pastorelli tells us his secret this way: "People in good health hardly realize that sickness can be the discovery of unknown resources in ourselves and in the circumstances of our life; it can be the overturning of many false values, and the encountering of true values face to face. Even if we tried to rise to the sheer, stark reality of what is essential, and pursued what we considered to be the only thing necessary, it is probable that this spiritual flight would be taken for an impoverished life by those in good health. Besides, sick or well, a being that spiritualizes itself lives in a zone that is invisible to those who are blinded by worldly pursuits. No matter what the case, the one who takes refuge in the center of his soul, and the one who lets his soul be blown about by every wind, do not evaluate life according to the same standard. However, sickness adds its particular factors to this. A host of human ambitions still constitute the essence of life for the greatest number of those in good health. Now sickness draws us into a region where we are forced to see the emptiness and worthlessness of these ambitions. Sickness teaches us to cast off from us, like a garment that is comfortable and valuable, perhaps, but useless, a world of vainglories and trifles that agitate and trouble our life without enriching or renovating it."

Suzanne Fouché, who was afflicted with coxalgia, noticed the same thing: "They understood that I would have to suffer and struggle, but no one imagined that I would have peace as well.

"My smile made them uneasy. Having scaled the wall, I find myself alone on the other side.

"We were never intimate before. How can I confide in them now? Our juxtaposed lives have no common denominator, and for the first time, I am suffering because only the surface waves of our beings have mingled, while the depths lay beyond reach.

"I say nothing, but my peace, my freedom of spirit are almost too eloquent: 'It's all the same to her,' says my father, shrugging his shoulders. They judge me quite unconcerned in accepting 'so easily'; they almost would accuse me of going to meet the ordeal.

"I let them suspect me of being unbalanced. What I have discovered on the other shore occupies me enough.

". . . Maybe I ought to have explained myself a little. But, how?

"Many times, when I heard a footstep at the door, I resolved to try to overthrow the wall that separated us, but I hadn't the courage to reveal myself and to give up the secret of my God. I know only too well with what a piteous tone the word 'mystic' would be said of me.

"I didn't want anyone to laugh at what God had done for me. . . ."

She emphasizes, moreover, another kind of misunderstanding:

"And my relatives' attitude is quite evident: 'My dear child, resign yourself to this ordeal'; their complete misunderstanding hurt me less than this well-meaning advice.

"To resign myself, to give in, to compromise—when it was never so necessary to possess myself and to struggle . . .

"God does not love a back bent beneath the rod. When

He held out the cross to me and I took it, it was done out of love, and it was with love that I committed myself to Him."

There is something striking about these accounts. They ought to make us infinitely more attentive and humble. A sick woman once told me: "You do your best to understand, but no one can understand . . ."

Whatever we do, we will never understand others completely, even by putting our whole heart and soul into it. There is a secret element in each one of us that is like no other. We desire to be reached as far as this inexpressible depth. But no one can penetrate that far. Only God.

13. *Insight*

For many of us, insight consists in not being outwitted by our neighbor, and in skillfully detecting his weak points, his little ruses, his lies, and his villainy.

Can we be so sure of our clear-sightedness? To really become lucid, would we not do better to fathom the depths of our own self with critical insight? There we might find obstacles that keep us aloof from our neighbor and prevent us from seeing him as he really is.

Let us examine three of the most prominent of these hindrances.

1. *The Tyranny of Labels*

One of the most diabolic obstacles of all is the tyranny of ideologies or labels.

We live in a world where real, concrete beings, men of flesh and blood like you and me, Joe and Josephine, are disappearing more and more, and giving way to abstract ideas, to systems, groups, cliques, and parties. When someone is spoken of today, it is no longer he that people are directly interested in, his person, or what he really is in himself. They rather want to know to what class, race, party, religion, and even profession he belongs. A man can no longer be reached except through the general or collective label we stick on him. He is an American or a foreigner, a Northerner or a Southerner, a factory worker or a white collar man, a Republican or a Democrat, a Catholic or a Protestant.

What are the regrettable consequences of this state of mind? Men are no longer known as they really are; they become abstractions to one another because of the mask we have put on them; they reproach and mutually despise each other, return injury for injury; and they do not make the slightest effort to meet one another in his individual and unique personality, to understand, help, or love one another.

It is characteristic of ideologies and parties to stress the things that divide them, and thus to exclude and combat each other.

On the contrary, it is the destiny of realistic men to approach and understand each other. Parties are bent on opposing each other, whereas men grow and develop by loving one another. I do not mean to say that we should not have personal ideas, or adhere to a system or a party; yet how desirable it would be if we showed our good will by trying to see how our doctrine is in harmony with another's, instead of just insisting on the things that divide us. Still, it is quite normal that all men do not think the same way as far as national, social, economic, or even religious problems are concerned.

However, the ideas to which a man adheres do not exhaust his whole personality, nor do they completely express him. You do not have to be a keen observer to notice, for instance, that in all the groups and parties that confront one another, men are extremely diverse. If I disregard the party differences, and go to the real persons, everywhere, along with those who are narrow-minded, unrefined, and egotistical, I find men who are frank, cultured, broad-minded, and generous. I can regret the fact that they do not think as I do about the organization of the country, of society, or religion, and I can try to win them over to my viewpoint; but since God has given them a concrete personality that is more precious than all the world, I must never cease loving them an instant. Moreover, when I ponder the fact that they have been redeemed by the blood of Christ and have an eternal and divine vocation just as I have, with what respect, with what attention and sincere affection ought I not consider and treat them?

Everyone knows the gospel scene in which the weary Christ stops at Jacob's well. Then along comes a Samaritan woman to draw water. Everyone knows that Jews and Samaritans never associate with one another. But Jesus says to her: "Give me to drink."

The Samaritan woman answers him: "How is it that thou, although thou art a Jew, dost ask drink of me, who am a Samaritan woman?"

You can see at once the labels: Jews and Samaritans. But the Divine Master is very far from such narrowness. In the woman before Him, He sees only an individual and real creature, whom He has come to save. Ignoring the barrier she raises, He begins speaking to her of the living water which He has come to give all His Father's creatures.

As for St. Paul, listen to him: "There is neither Jew nor Greek, nor slave nor free man ... You are but one in Christ."

Everyone who has the sense of man and whose mind is not warped by ideologies or clouded by prejudices understands this instinctively. There is, for instance, the Bishop of Liége and many other priests and laymen who gave refuge to persecuted Jews during the war. Another striking example of this was given by some Belgian coal miners who deprived themselves of their dinner during the war for Russian prisoners. That's very natural, you will say. They were allies. True, but after the war, they did the same thing for other prisoners, who were yesterday's enemies, the Germans who worked with them in the mines. Do you not find this a hundred times more human than hatred?

We will only be saved if the leaven of unity and love rises in us to conquer the barriers which systems, parties, and races have set up between human beings.

Without a doubt, work and production are important today to save our country and the world. But there is also a need among all men for the constant will to tear off these labels and so find what they have been hiding from us—the real human person, the brother, the companion of eternity. "Men should never be judged according to the categories to which they belong. The category is the most barbarous and diabolical aberration ever born of man's brain. We must not forget that even our enemy is a man and not a category."

2. Adversaries

A second obstacle that keeps us from understanding and reaching men is that ensemble of instinctive reactions we have towards those who oppose us. Our adversaries are those of the other side. But couldn't anyone become our adversary in life? Tomorrow our dearest friend, perhaps! And all because of a party line!

Then we shut all doors to understanding, and blinding passions surge up in us. Instead of saying to ourselves, "Watch out; now's the time to guard your feelings, reactions, judgments, and the words with which you express them," we let ourselves be dominated by our instincts of defense, and by all the aggressive powers latent in us. We make judgments that are radical, narrow-minded, over-simplified, and distorted; and we state them in a sharp, absolute, and dogmatic way. And so we divide the world into two camps: on the one side, the good, the perfect, the just, the true, the sincere and upright: we and those who think like us; on the other side, the evil, the common, the hypocrites, the perverse, the false, the corrupt, in short, all those who oppose us.

Is this an exaggeration? Think of what goes on about you every day. Everyone is complaining that the spirit of justice, truth, courtesy, and fair play is vanishing. But, because of an odd blindness, they always notice this disappearance only in the opposite camp. Hypocrisy, treachery, and bad faith are always in others.

And do not think that it's just ordinary men or hurried journalists who act like this: you can find serious persons, sensible in most of their judgments, learned men and professors who are scrupulously objective in all that touches scientific research, but who, once it is a question of political, social, national, or world affairs, make judgments that are impassioned, deformed, and harmful.

Canon Jacques Leclercq shows how this deformation is found even among those who are habitually animated by the highest charity: "So many charitable men," he writes, "who are working for the good of others, are hard and unjust if ever a question of class or party arises in their work; they condemn with arrogance, without even dreaming of finding out what is going on in the other man's mind."

How can we explain such aberrations? One explanation is this: once we are partisans, we become poor observers, we notice in others only what favors our position. Everything our opponent says or writes we listen to or read with an unconscious care to find fault with it and refute it. How often have you seen men in public discussions whose primary concern was only to find ideas in their opponent's words which could correct, complete, modify, or mitigate their own ideas? Hardly ever! We usually find men who are always searching for ways to preserve their own notions. Unconsciously, they filter their opponent's speech, retaining just the weak points, which they then isolate from all the rest.

Also (and this is the worst of all—and a frequent occurrence) we find men accusing their opponents of a bad action which they, at that very minute, are committing themselves. There is the politician who complains that some one has slandered him, and to that very complaint, he couples the rudest injuries. Christ already put us on guard against this danger: "Why dost thou see the speck in thy brother's eye, and yet dost not consider the beam in thine own eye?"

The reason is that we observe our neighbor more easily than we do ourselves. We have him before our eyes, and we see him without any trouble. We almost have to cut ourselves in two in order to see the truth about us in all its reality.

Let us not forget that we are in the habit of judging ourselves after the ideal we profess, and not after our actual realization of it. We judge our intentions, and not our actions. But when it comes to judging our opponents, we follow quite a different course. Far from looking at their intentions, we judge them from their actions alone. Now, these are always more or less open to suspicion. It is never hard to oppose a man's actions to his intentions.

3. *Bad Faith*

Finally, we must avoid accusing others too quickly of bad faith. There is hardly a more frequent accusation in political speeches and newspaper columns. Along with the words *treachery* and *hypocrisy,* the expression *bad faith* makes up part of the current vocabulary when political passions blind both mind and heart. Since this idea is worth considering, let us clarify the matter by distinguishing two kinds of bad faith: conscious bad faith and unconscious bad faith.

Conscious bad faith consists in deceiving our neighbor knowingly and systematically. It is a lie in its pure state, if I may use such an expression.

Is this self-conscious and therefore brazen and cynical bad faith very frequent? I do not think so. Man is so used to deceiving himself that he is usually unconscious of deceiving others. When it is a question of himself, or the defense of his ideology or party, it becomes an unimaginable blindness.

The most striking example is that of criminals who sincerely believe they are gentle and beneficent men. Dale Carnegie cites the case of the famous gangster, "Two Gun" Crowley, who was arrested in New York on May 7, 1931, after one of the most sensational man-hunts the city had ever known. Not less than one hundred and fifty police-men and detectives, armed with machine guns, were needed to capture him in the apartment where he had taken refuge. When Crowley was captured, the Police Commissioner "declared that the two-gun desperado was one of the most dangerous criminals ever encountered in the history of New York. 'He will kill,' said the Commissioner, 'at the drop of a feather.' Now while this gun battle was raging, Crowley wrote a letter addressed 'To whom it may concern.' In this letter he said: 'Under my coat is a weary heart, but a kind one—one that would do nobody any harm.'

"A short time before this, Crowley had been having a necking party on a country road out on Long Island. Suddenly a policeman walked up to the parked car and said: 'Let me see your license.'

"Without saying a word, Crowley drew his gun, and cut the policeman down with a shower of lead. As the dying officer fell, Crowley leaped out of the car, grabbed the officer's revolver, and fired another bullet into the prostrate body. And that was the killer who said: 'Under my coat is a weary heart, but a kind one—one that would do nobody any harm.'

"Crowley was sentenced to the electric chair. When he arrived at the death house at Sing Sing, did he say, 'This is what I get for killing people.'? No, he said: 'This is what I get for defending myself.' " [1]

Conscious bad faith? I don't think so. Good faith, then? Hardly!

I expressly chose an extreme case because it illustrates very graphically what unconscious bad faith can be like. But we can find the same phenomenon in thousands of men. Who, moreover, would dare say he had never fallen into this kind of bad faith?

What should we do to escape it, to be cured of these

[1] *How to Win Friends and Influence People.*

illusions, and leave this subjective but "false sincerity" to return to a truly good faith? First of all, we ought to reflect upon ourselves, take a good look, judge, and set to work clarifying, purifying, and illuminating ourselves. Quite often we unfortunately prefer to be blind in this regard, and if, by chance, we have a qualm of conscience, we quickly turn aside our attention. Instinctively we dread the demands it will make, and so we thwart it. We prefer to live in a semi-conscious state, in half obscurity, instead of keeping our conscience awake and clear. So it is that we develop shadowed areas in us that become more and more opaque, enveloping our sincerity in a kind of fog. We think we are still sincere, whereas in reality we have already turned our back on the truth.

True sincerity is not natural to man; it is a hard, daily, hourly struggle. Insight is only acquired at the price of a severe and ceaseless combat.

14. *Seventy Times Seven*

How hard it is to forgive and do it well!

"I can forgive, but I can't forget." How often we hear that. Certainly, we cannot forget everything we would like to. But we are required to quench and strip our remembrance of every grudge. If it remains branded with bitterness, it is a sign that we have not truly forgiven.

When we read the Gospel, we cannot fail to be struck by Christ's insistence in teaching this difficult law of forgiveness.

He makes it an absolutely necessary condition for God's pardon of our own faults. He makes us say in the Our Father: "Forgive us our trespasses as we forgive those who trespass against us." And St. Matthew's Gospel adds immediately: "For if you forgive men their offenses, your heavenly Father will also forgive you your offenses. But if you do not forgive men, neither will your Father forgive you your offenses."

And we read in St. Mark: "And when you stand up to pray, forgive whatever you have against anyone, that your Father in heaven may also forgive you your offenses."

Finally, there is the parable of the king who demands an accounting. Discovering that one of his servants owes him an important sum, he condemns him to the confiscation of all his property. But the man begs pardon, and the king releases him from his debt. Yet, no sooner has he gone out than he lays hold of one of his own debtors—a man who is indebted to him for a much smaller sum. The wicked servant listens to neither his excuses nor his pleas, but has him thrown into prison. Learning of this, the king changes his mind and inflicts the same punishment on the wicked servant: "So also my heavenly Father will do to you, if you do not each forgive your brothers from your hearts."

This insistence ought to make us reflect. Forgiveness appears in the Gospel as the perfection of the law of love. In it should lie hidden secret values that are without a doubt among the richest of Christianity, yet the most unacknowledged by pagans and by Christians themselves.

Let us try to discover them. The first thing we see is that forgiveness, to be really sincere, demands a great victory over our instincts. When someone has offended, wounded, humiliated, or outraged our person, our possessions, our honor, our convictions, or our affections, the hoard of passions that lie dormant deep down in our being rise up tumultuously in revolt.

First of all, there is the instinct of self-defense. Anyone who has wronged me appears as a danger—an enemy against whom I ought to protect myself. Instinctive sentiments of distrust, fear, and antipathy arise in me. Spontaneously I am on my guard against him.

Now, to forgive is to go beyond this simply defensive attitude, however natural and sound it may seem. Naturally, I should not have any illusions as to the strength of the one who wishes to harm or do me wrong. I must do what is necessary to protect myself. But I may not stop there. I ought to master this fear in me, and rest assured that what is best in me is beyond the reach of my enemy. I must reinforce my inner personality. In fact, the more disposed a man is to magnanimity and forgiveness, the more will he feel intimately secure and sheltered from every harm. To be constantly on the defensive is a sign of weakness. One who truly forgives reveals more spiritual power than one who fears and hates.

This is why the saints forgave so easily. How can the opinions, criticisms, injuries, even the services of others hurt them? Their treasure is out of reach. They enjoy that marvelous inner freedom we find to the highest degree in Christ.

Jesus is the true examplar of forgiveness. Judas betrays Him, yet He reproves him gently. The Apostles doze, and He reproaches them tenderly. A servant slaps Him; He answers him calmly and nobly. Peter denies Him, and Jesus looks upon him with love. The soldiers crucify Him; He says: "Father, forgive them." We feel that He is like an impregnable fortress in the face of men, a solitude that is not accessible, a world that cannot be troubled.

Furthermore, to forgive I must silence in me the desire for vengeance, the instinct for reprisals, the "eye-for-an-eye" tendency. Romano Guardini has carefully analyzed what happens within us when someone has hurt us: "The fact that the other was able to damage me proves that he was stronger than I; had I been what I should be, he never would have dared to attempt it. The impulse to retaliate aims primarily at reestablishing my self-respect by humiliating my enemy. I would rise by the other's fall . . . To forgive him would mean to renounce this satisfaction, and necessitates a self-respect independent of the behavior of others because it lives from an intrinsic honor that is invulnerable." [1]

Did not St. Teresa of Avila say that if she received a slap on the face, it would cause her no more emotion than if a little plaster had fallen from the ceiling?

All well and good, you will say, but isn't forgiveness contrary to justice? When someone has slighted me, order has been disturbed. Isn't it quite necessary that I try to reestablish it? Doubtlessly. But guided by what? By the instinct of justice or by the virtue of justice? The confusion is so general, as we have seen, that it is a good idea to return to this point and clarify it more.

The instinct of justice drives me to treat another as he treats me. It is the law of retaliation: "An eye for an eye, a tooth for a tooth." The virtue of justice, however, wills that the other be treated according to his real guilt, or else I am worth no more than he, and fall into injustice as he has fallen.

[1] *The Lord*

The instinct of justice usually acts under the influence of passion, and involves thoughtless actions and hasty executions. The virtue of justice is carried out with calmness and self-control; it leans on reason for support; it examines everything and judges carefully.

During the war, a Belgian, Paul Levy, was in the concentration camp at Breendonck, a prisoner of the SS-man Schmitt, the cruel leader of the camp. By a singular turn of events, Paul Levy himself was later sent to go and get his former tormentor at the prison in Rotterdam, and bring him back for trial in Belgium.

He later related: "I was insulted by the driver of the staff car who brought us back, because I had given Schmitt something to eat; by a security officer, because I had not raised a hand against him; and by another, because I was concerned for his natural needs, and made them stop the car so he could take care of these—something which he had often hindered us from doing at Breendonck. Since that time many have said to me: 'You fool—you should have killed him!' I thought it enough to reply that I was no Nazi."

What a beautiful victory of the virtue of justice over the instinct of justice! But such victories are rare.

The instinct of justice, as we have seen, drives a man on to do himself justice. The virtue of justice leaves this concern to the established authorities: the state, destiny, and, in the end, God. It knows very well that we are driven to exaggerate another's wrongs and that the only true judge is one who has not been involved.

The instinct of justice delights in the chastisement of the guilty. What leads the masses to accept capital punishment? The pure joy of seeing violated order restored? Hardly!

Rather, it is the base pleasure of seeing injury rendered for injury, suffering for suffering, and death for death!

The virtue of justice does not delight in these equivalences. It looks upon the guilty man as one to save rather than as one to chastise. Surely it must guard society against his crimes, but, at the same time, it should do all it can to make him realize his guilt, regret his fault, and regain his taste for an upright and worthy life.

How sad it is to find human justice so far removed from this spirit, especially during and after a war—even in the most civilized countries!

If Christ has so insistently demanded the forgiveness of offenses, it is undoubtedly because He saw in this the surest testimony of true love and authentic charity.

By it, we see in every man a creature of God, and we see that our mission is to make as much good as possible develop and bloom in his personality. Once we have understood this, instead of suffering from injuries received, we will rather suffer because we see our neighbor doing wrong. The victim is not the one to be pitied most, but the culprit.

Generally, we can only arrive at the summit of love if we keep very near to Christ, and so participate in His inner liberty, His total security, His creative bounty, His expiative and redemptive mission. Like Him, we no longer think of anything except saving that which is lost.

If there are so few Christians who have the spirit of forgiveness, it is because they live too far from God and their brothers; they are lost in the labyrinth of their egotistical reactions.

Yet without the greatness that forgiveness requires, life is very hard to live. We have to forgive even those who love us best "seventy times seven" for their lack of attention, their forgetfulness, their provocations, touchiness, harsh words; and we must accept the fact that they are different from us, and profoundly inaccessible and incomprehensible.

Then, who knows, if one day we shall not be suddenly placed in a situation where forgiveness will be especially difficult and at the same time necessary. I am thinking of all those who are victims of some grave injustice in their social life, or some treason in their married life, or some terrible ordeal in paternal or maternal love. Think of the mother whose child has been murdered, or the parents whose honor and happiness are darkened by the misconduct of a son or a daughter. Then it is really hard to keep our heart and arms wide open, and be the one to plead, to make the necessary advances, and, if pushed away ten times, to make it known ten times more that we are always ready to welcome the guilty person and help him regain his former dignity.

Yet there are some who do climb to the summit, and this is one of the most moving sights one can imagine. The year Belgium was liberated, a Lenten preacher chose charity as his subject.

One Saturday afternoon, one of his fellow priests came to see him: "You know I'm stationed at the military prison. Well, there are some Gestapo officers there who have not had a change of clothing for a year. Since you're preaching on charity, I thought you might ask if someone would be willing to give me some clothes for them."

Next day, he passed on his friend's appeal to his congregation, adding this simple comment: "My brothers, you will probably think: 'These men have done us wrong.' I simply recall to you the words of our Lord: 'If you are my disciples, you will do good even to those who do you wrong.'"

Monday morning, the first bundles arrived. In one of them were four shirts along with this letter:

"Dear Father, I am a poor woman. I had two sons. The elder was killed in the war. The other was arrested by the Gestapo and taken to prison. He died there of suffering and cold.

"I have kept these four shirts as relics of my poor boy. But yesterday I heard your sermon, I heard your appeal and the words from the Gospel with which you closed.

"So this morning I'm sending you these four shirts for the German prisoners."

Then, too, there is the example given by the mayor of Toledo, Spain, who was executed in 1936 by the Communists. Before his death, he asked his wife and children to forgive his executioners and to aid them if they ever needed help later on.

Finally, remember the mother of St. Maria Goretti greeting her daughter's assassin upon his release from prison, and giving public proof of her forgiveness by going to Communion with the penitent!

Few things make us more like God than forgiveness!

15. *Have Faith in Man*

"Ah, yes, mankind is a wonderful thing, always wonderful. If only we had faith in mankind; if we would only believe in mankind all the time and in spite of everything! Just think for a while of all the good that has been done on this earth in the last two thousand years, and that would not have been done if Christ had not faith in mankind . . .

". . . if you say goodbye to the hope of human perfectibility, you may as well say goodbye to life at the same time. For then there is nothing left in this world. Nothing but struggle, killing, and making merry before killing oneself. No more humanity; no more conscience or duty or morals or civilization. If a man does not believe he can save his brothers, he is lost. One must die or save. It's the password to life." [1]

A password that is difficult to realize, for man is often discouraging to man. After trying to create good, to lift up spirits, and tear hearts from mediocrity and baseness, many men, even social or religious apostles, see their faith in man shaken and disappear. They seem to become sceptics. Their words betray great disillusionment; they willingly let themselves become bitter, critical, and abusive. This marks the end of their creative influence in the world. Without knowing it, they have joined forces with those who discourage hearts, make lives gloomy, and snap off the reed that is already bending low.

"Do not put out the wick that still smoulders," demands Christ. In every soul there always remains a spark, a glow, an aspiration toward good. Absolute evil does not exist in man. Sometimes he seems to be malice incarnate; but as soon as we come nearer to his soul, we can find some healthy parts and traces of grace there. Many need only someone to have faith in what good is in them.

What is, sometimes, more discouraging than evil itself is universal mediocrity. We are so aware of others' limitations that we sense a wall there that will never be knocked down.

[1] Maxence van der Meersch, *Bodies and Souls*.

And it never will be, as long as we continue to think that way. Faith is what changes the world—the conviction that man can be made more perfect, the sureness that in casting all our creative powers into the furnace, something worthwhile will come of it. The world has a great need of men who encourage their fellowmen.

Unfortunately, we see just the opposite. Together with irony, the craze to tear down someone else is one of the most common and detestable tendencies in the world.

We might say that most men are insensible to good, and that their antennas are only set for evil's wave length: they only pick up what is bad. This is basically due to the sadistic element in their souls—a sort of complacency in their own evil. Men should always be on guard against this. But instead, they try to nourish it every way possible.

Writers accept the axiom that it is impossible to write good literature about virtue. An author may have great talent, but let him choose his subject in a sphere other than that of unbridled and exultant passions, and he is sure of being classed at once among second-rate writers. It goes without saying that a novelist is free to choose his subjects in the world of reality, but why reserve it exclusively to evil, unless evil will attract more readers and pay off best.

The same holds true for the press. Its success is in direct proportion to the scandals it reports and its spirit of detraction. "Virtue, even heroism, interests only a small number of the public," wrote a journalist. "A nice crime excites the masses, including the elite, whereas the story of an honest man hardly pleases them at all; the story of an upright woman, not at all. I used to describe various aspects of virtue in the newspapers. I even christened this headline, 'The Good Folk,' and in it I related all sorts of noble deeds men have

done: life-saving, returning lost articles, hidden devotion
. . . But I soon found out that my litany of honors was interesting no one; it was thrown out to make room for the gory details of some nice crime. With this, the paper's circulation, which had fallen off, now began to increase."

We know how systematic the detraction of the papers can be. They know very well that they are catering to one of the evil tendencies in their readers. And they go right ahead, for it is so easy. Nothing is so simple as to destroy. Nothing is easier than the job of the writer who scribbles away and reforms the world each morning, while seated comfortably at his office. He never has a decision to make, a decree to sign; he never has to make a real choice between parties, never has to take into account anyone else's opinion or opposition. He just writes words, and that's all—he has no responsibility.

Detraction is one of the poisons most dangerous to social life. It kills good will. It makes it very difficult for those who try to keep their chin up. It sows suspicion, doubt, and scepticism.

Most men need to be encouraged. Many who outwardly appear sure of themselves secretly suffer from an inferiority complex. They doubt the quality of their decisions, the value of their influence, and the worth of their actions.

"The way to develop the best that is in a man is by appreciation and encouragement," wrote Charles Schwab, right hand man of the steel king, Andrew Carnegie. "There is nothing else that so kills the ambitions of a man as criticisms from his superiors. I never critize anyone. I believe in giving a man incentive to work. So I am anxious to praise, but loath to find fault. If I like anything, I am hearty in my approbation and lavish in my praise." [2]

[2] Cited by Dale Carnegie in *How to Win Friends and Influence People*.

Praise is often the sign of a soul with quality. We must be good ourselves to be able to see good in others, to rejoice in their good, to take pleasure in making it known round about us. Like everything, the value of praise can become corrupted, can degenerate into indiscretion, vulgarity, and flattery. But when it is the outpouring of a sincere heart, it is one of the most beautiful gifts we can offer someone. Praise makes one expand, blossom. It enkindles a new flame in his heart; it makes him live in an atmosphere of warmth and joy.

Men like to be congratulated for their work, their success in undertakings. And women generally know how to do it.

Women love to be praised, even more so than men. The latter, sad to say, for the most part are perfectly ignorant when it comes to giving compliments.

While courting, they think of it more. But once they are married, they become distracted and forgetful. Infatuated by their masculine egotism, professional life, and indifferent attitude, husbands neglect to take note of the thousand and one things wives do to please them.

However, there are exceptions.

I have great admiration, for instance, for the delicate art with which a great historian, Henri Pirenne, associated his wife with his great scientific work. In the preface of his *Histoire de Belgique,* he writes: "And now I say farewell to this work which has taken up a great part of my life and made it a great joy. During those thirty-five years, good health and the loving care of my dear wife kept me going. Without her tender cooperation, I would have never arrived at my goal."

16. *Satan Laughs*

THERE are all kinds of laughter . . .

There is the kind of laughter someone once called "God's music."

You hear it in a playground, in a kindergarten, at a teenagers' party, or you will hear it among novices at recreation.

There is also the kind of laugh people call *humorous,* which consists essentially in laughing at oneself and emphasizing the comical side of the situations in which one is involved—even though they be a bit tragic.

In certain instances, humor can be excessive, childish, and irritating. Held within its limits, it keeps us from appearing too solemn to others, and too god-like to ourselves. It also comes to us just in the nick of time to bridle our tendency to dramatize trifles; and when there really is tragedy, humor reduces it to its proper proportions and helps us keep our inner faculties under control so that we can face the situation.

But there is another type of laughter which has rightly been called by Lamartine "one of the evil faculties of our soul."

This is ridicule.

Ridicule is often a sign of spiritual indigence. But not

always, for there are mockers who do have wit: Voltaire, for instance. But mockery always is an indigence of soul. It shows a lack of seriousness toward life, and especially a total disregard for the person and the human drama that evolves in consciences, even in those that appear the most frivolous and light-headed.

In many cases irony is the sign of pride and pretension. Bossuet wrote, "The victory of pride is irony." "An ironical spirit is always looking for tiny flaws in people and things, noting how they fall short of their ideal, and sizing up in a glance what they are and what they ought to be. He looks upon humanity and nature as the uncorrected note-book of a poor student. Thus he affirms his knowledge, insight, and superiority. He builds himself up as a 'court of no-appeal.' And his behavior betrays the good opinion he has of himself."

The ironic soul is superficial and fickle. Everything in this world has an eternal side and a funny side, but the mocker grasps only the funny side. He never penetrates to the core of things. He sees only their secondary aspects. "The pleasure of criticism robs us of the joy of being deeply moved by some of the loveliest things." This is very true. The man who is perpetually looking for something funny or witty is never moved with deep emotion. He thinks he sees clearly, whereas he goes through life a blind man. "This is why I hate irony, for it is not worthy of a man, but of a dunce."

Basically, irony does nothing but degrade. It never constructs anything. It only destroys. The mocker is often a very weak character who, stripped of any creative abilities, gives way to his destructive tendencies. "Not everyone has the strength to raise a monument, but everyone has the strength to wrench away a block, a stone, or a pebble from another's monument."

Undoubtedly we can use irony to make vice look ridiculous. Scripture itself gives us examples of this, and literature has found there an immense domain to exploit. It is likewise perfectly legitimate to combat all tyranny and unjust oppression by laughing it off, as during the war.

Finally, when a man does some foolish thing which is obviously harmful, we may very well undermine his influence by making fun of it. Charity demands that we protect the innocent and the weak, even if it be at the expense of the guilty party. Even then, we must preserve justice and moderation, a thing that is difficult and not too common.

Ridicule is a vice that is extremely widespread in our civilization. It is rarely found among Oriental peoples, who are of a more serious and sedate nature.

What makes this vice especially dangerous is that its malice escapes the notice of many. For a great many men, to show one's wit at the expense of a neighbor or to ridicule him is to prove one's intelligence—almost one's virtue. . . . Isn't this a good way to amuse your audience? Do you not render your neighbor an outstanding service by making him see the faults which enslave him? Even some parents and teachers favor joking, irony, and ridicule as an excellent method of education.

Certainly, there is a playful and slightly pleasant tone that reveals a deep affection, and is always encouraging. But, if there is an attitude that baffles a child or an adolescent, that creates in him an uneasiness, kills his confidence, makes him close in on himself, and at times fosters in him the deepest grudges, it is ridicule! If we are not on our guard, we easily fall victims to mockery. All we have to do is let our lower nature speak for itself, and off we go.

Look at little children. Sometimes, even when they are very young, they have group reactions when they are together that lead them to pick on one of their small playmates who is weaker, clumsier, or perhaps afflicted in some way.

Some adolescents, at the "silly stage," make fun (and what fun!) of everything and everybody. They do not see how ridiculous they are themselves, and they keep up the nonsense which they alone find funny and laugh at with a joyless humor.

Many of them find their equilibrium and seriousness again later on. But others persist in pursuing the ridiculous, and become inveterate windbags, who in the eyes of the rest of men have a perpetual itch for something to laugh at. It is not rare that we see them sink to the ranks of the jokers, scorners, sceptics, bitter men, and go through life pouring out their spite in clubs, discussion groups, or periodicals.

What can be said for orators and journalists who mock and slander the reviews of their critics, and who stoop so low as to ridicule the physique of their opponents or the manner in which they dress?

When we have seen closely the ravages wrought by ridicule in a soul, we cannot but become its bitter enemy.

For my part, I remember a certain inaccessible, morose, and touchy pupil who seemed to bristle like a fortress. One day while I was correcting one of his compositions, I discovered the answer to the riddle. For a year, he had had a teacher who had never stopped making fun of him. I later found out that this teacher had meant no harm and really liked this pupil as much as the others. But unfortunately, he had succeeded in creating in this young lad, who was gifted moreover with real qualities and generous aspirations, an absolute defiance and frightful bitterness toward his teacher.

I remember another boy whose excessive timidity made

him very ill at ease. As a result, he had gone through school haunted by the ridicule of his schoolmates. They never knew how much they aggravated his innate timidity and humiliated him in his own eyes. They convinced him that he would never amount to anything, whereas he was not really lacking in talent or intelligence.

"You won't believe it," he later told me, "but there were days when I suffered so much that I thought of suicide."

Wasn't Christ thinking of ridicule when He said: "Woe to you who laugh!"

17. *The Forces That Create Me*

Love is essentially creative. When it fills a being, it wants to overflow into other beings. It tends to make them exist, at least to make them flourish and grow. Philosophers say, "The *I* is awakened thanks to the *Thou.*" This is rigorously true in God, where the Persons exist only because of an absolute reciprocity, the Father being a person only because of the Son, and the Son only because of the Father, and the Holy Ghost because of the love that binds them. Three pure reciprocities which communicate in the same, unique, divine reality! Three loves which give each other this reality mutually, which have it only because they receive it from another, and are persons only because they are pure altruism! Forgetfulness of self! Regard for the "Other"! Giving! Communion! Love! All this takes on in God such purity that our intellect staggers, dazzled and stammering, yet happy because it fathoms here love in its supreme form and knows it is called to participate in this mystery.

There are people in the world who do not want to be indebted to anyone. They are too proud, they will tell you. Without a doubt, there are innumerable ways the world would like to enslave us, and we must stay free from them, but we all depend on one another, and on God. One would have to be blind not to see this. Are *we* blind?

We are more impressed in our life by what we do than by what we undergo. Our actions stand out in broad daylight before our conscience and memory. We can easily enumerate what we did yesterday and what we plan to do today.

As to the influences working upon us—that is quite another story. They remain in the semi-darkness of our consciousness, especially when they are in full harmony with our being and cooperate in our physical, intellectual, moral, or spiritual growth. At every moment, I am aided, sustained, and formed by these elements, by men and by God. I am at the crossroads of a thousand creative forces. I receive in me much more than I create myself. Yet I forget it!

To discover these happy influences, I must do some systematic reflexion. I must light my lantern and penetrate into the vague darkness to find the forces that create me. Then, with St. Francis of Assisi, I will be able to say:

"Most high, almighty, and kind Lord,

To Thee is all praise, honor and glory, all benediction;

Be Thou praised, my Lord, with all Thy creatures."

Then we will profit from such an occasion and tell our parents, our relatives, our old school teachers, and our friends, discreetly and delicately, just how much we owe them—even those who seem to have only received from us, for we never give without receiving from them. Life is an exchange, a communion. No one enters deeply within us to sup there without bringing something precious with him at the same time: himself. This is the essential, be he the poorest of creatures! For there is a world in each one. We are aware of this each time that a soul, tearing away its mask, dares to be completely open to us.

Gratitude is one of the gifts our neighbor most appreciates. It produces in him a mysterious impression of light, growth, and blossoming. Léon Bloy, who had a deep sense of the mystery of human relationship and communion, wrote: "When my little girl calls me 'Daddy,' it seems to me that my kingdom has come."

To be given well and to be well received, gratitude demands great purity and simplicity.

Simone Weil wrote: "If the gift is rightly given and rightly received, the passing of a morsel of bread from one man to another is something like a real communion."

The same can be said for gratitude. Given well, received well, it constitutes a deep exchange where God's is implicitly present.

Gratitude, as was said, is a rare thing. I would like to pluck from it an exquisite flower born in a pagan soil— the Emperor Marcus Aurelius.

We can certainly regret that he was hard on the Christians. But he was in good faith, very likely. For at that time the State dominated everything and Christians were considered a danger to the Empire. But as he reveals himself in his writings, Marcus Aurelius appears as one of the noblest souls in pagan antiquity.

The first book of his *Meditations* is undoubtedly the most beautiful song of gratitude that has ever poured forth from a human heart. With a gem cutter's grace, he recalls and enumerates in a striking manner the things he admires most in those who had been about him, and all that he owes to his parents, educators, friends, and gods.

In the following quotation, we have given the main passages where he exalts goodness, gentleness, and affection.

"From my grandfather Verus: a kindly disposition and sweetness of temper.

"From what I heard of my father and my memory of him: modesty and manliness.

"From my mother: the fear of God, and generosity; and abstention, not only from doing ill, but even from the very thought of doing it; and furthermore to lead the simple life, far removed from the habits of the rich.

"From my tutor: not to side with the Green Jacket or the Blue at the races, or to back the Light-Shield Champion or the Heavy-Shield in the lists [. . . the colors and weapons by which one designated the rival troupes of riders and gladiators in the Circus], not to shirk toil, and to have few wants, and to do my own work, and to mind my own concerns, and to turn a deaf ear to slander.

"From Rusticus: to become aware of the fact that I needed amendment and training for my character . . . not to pose ostentatiously as the moral athlete or unselfish man . . . to show myself ready to be reconciled to those who have lost their temper and trespassed against one, and ready to meet them halfway as soon as ever they seem to be willing to retrace their steps.

"From Apollonius: to remain ever the same, in the throes of pain, on the loss of a child, during a lingering illness; and to see plainly from a living example that one and the same man can be very vehement and yet gentle; not to be impatient in instructing others; and to learn in accepting seeming favors from friends not to give up our independence for such things nor take them callously as a matter of course.

"From Sextus: kindliness, and the example of a household patriarchally governed . . . and an intuitive consideration for friends; and a toleration of the unlearned and the unreasoning. . . . And never to exhibit any symptom of anger or any other passion, but to be at the same time utterly impervious to all passions and full of affection; and to praise without noisy obtrusiveness, and to possess great learning, but make no parade of it.

"From Alexander the Grammarian: not to love to criticize. . . .

"From Fronto: to note the envy, the subtlety, and the dissimulation which are habitual to a tyrant; and that, as a general rule, those amongst us who rank as patricians are somewhat wanting in natural affection.

"From Alexander the Platonist: not to say to anyone often or without necessity, nor to write in a letter, 'I am too busy,' nor in this fashion constantly to plead urgent affairs as an excuse for evading the obligations entailed upon us by our relations toward those around us.

"From Catulus: not to disregard a friend's expostulation even when it is unreasonable, but to try to bring him back to his usual friendliness; and to speak with whole-hearted good will of one's teachers.

"From my 'brother' Severus: love of family, love of truth, love of justice . . . and readiness to do others a kindness, and eager generosity, and optimism, and confidence in the love of friends . . . and the absence of any need for his friends to surmise what he did or did not wish, so plain was it.

"From my father [Emperor Antoninus, his uncle and

step-father]: mildness, and an unshakable adherence to decisions deliberately come to; and no empty vanity in respect to so-called honors ... but most of all a readiness to acknowledge without jealousy the claims of those who were endowed with any special gift, such as eloquence or knowledge of the law or ethics or any other subject ... there was nothing rude in him, nor yet overbearing or violent nor carried, as the phrase goes, 'to the sweating state.'

"From the Gods: to have good grandfathers, good parents, a good sister, good teachers, good companions, kinsmen, friends—nearly all of them; and that I fell into no trespass against any of them, and yet I had a disposition that way inclined, such as might have led me into something of the sort, had it been so chanced ... and that I kept unstained the flower of my youth; and that I did not make trial of my manhood before the due time, but even postponed it ... that it was my lot to have such a brother, capable by his character of stimulating me to watchful care over myself, and at the same time delighting me by his deference and affection ... that my mother, though she was to die young, yet spent her last years with me. That as often as I had the inclination to help anyone, who was in pecuniary distress or needing any other assistance, I was never told that there was no money available for the purpose ... that I have been blessed with a wife so docile, so affectionate, and so unaffected."[1]

[1] Marcus Aurelius Antoninus, *Meditations* ("The Loeb Classical Library," LVIII [Cambridge, Mass.: Harvard University Press]).

18. *Charity Is Not Provoked*

THERE is a well-known story about Alexander of Macedonia and his friend Clitus. Once Clitus had saved Alexander's life. Then, later on, during the course of a dinner, Clitus indulged in a little jesting at the king's expense. The king, stung to the quick, became so angry that he snatched a spear from the hands of a guard and ran him through.

Countless are the crimes due to anger. The newspapers carry proof enough of this. Yet, even if anger does not lead to murder, it is so opposed to the respect and love we owe our neighbor, and does men so much harm, that we can see very clearly why Christ was so severe in speaking of it.

"You have heard that it was said to the men of old, thou shalt not kill; if a man kills, he must answer for it before the court of justice. But I tell you that any man who is angry with his brother must answer for it before the court of justice, and any man who says Raca [empty-headed] to his brother must answer for it before the Council; and any man who says to his brother, thou fool, must answer for it in hell fire."

In the face of this insistence, we sense that Christ, here as always, wants to protect precious values from the violence that lies dormant within each of us.

First He wants to protect us against ourselves. To begin

with, anger is actually a lack of self-respect. Few things make a man less human than anger. Every passion that runs wild and unbridled makes an animal of man. Anger turns him into a blind force, like the unchained fury that nature's elements sometimes become. In a fit of violent anger, we might say, there is nothing left of the man. Just recall the red, distorted face, the wild, blood-shot eyes, the choked words, the stamping feet, all the insults, curses, vain threats, and absurd demands.

"I was beside myself," he will say later. "I couldn't get hold of myself; I lost all self-control." It's quite true. Anger loosens the steering-wheel we have to guide ourselves. For the time being, we cease to be men.

Queen Mary of Rumania tells in her *Memoirs* how one day, when still a young girl, her mother went for a stroll with Lady Mary, a woman whom both she and her two sisters disliked because of some slander they had heard about her from their governess.

The three young girls had a pony, and their mother asked if one of them would loan her pony to Lady Mary, to go up a steep path. They refused under the pretext that the animal was too small for a grown-up. But their mother insisted.

"It was then," relates the Queen, "that the regrettable scene took place. We were furious; and while we climbed the hill behind mother and Lady Mary on our pony, we began to throw insults at her and her daughters, who were also riding along in a carriage. Heaven only knows how we insulted their mother in front of those poor girls. All our governess' unjust slander came pouring out. At the top of the hill, Lady Mary dismounted and the pony was returned to its owner. To show her indignation at our rudeness, mother walked ahead with her guest without even looking at us.

"At that, we started in again—worse than ever, as if oil had been poured on the fire of our rage. Smothering our sobs, like three wild beasts abandoned by God and men, we rode down the hill, galloping at full speed. From behind the carriage we shrieked and stuck out our tongues at Lady Mary—at the same time shouting the vilest epithets in our repertoire, fortunately a very limited one. . . ."

And the narrator makes this exact observation:

"At certain moments in life we doubtlessly experience a bitter lowering of the flood gates to let out our resentment as if to bathe ourselves in it; but only sadness and humiliation is the result. When we are back to normal, we realize the indiscretion and shamefulness of our outburst. Our anger is followed by shame and dejection."

Anger is also a lack of respect for others. It assumes that they have bad intentions, even though they are very often just weak, incapable, or clumsy. Even if others are at fault, anger exaggerates, gets dramatic, and is unfair. It kicks at animals or inanimate things that cannot be to blame. It strikes and injures men who do not deserve to be punished. Even men, who are usually inclined to be just, who normally would not harm anyone at all, commit crying injustices and become hard and cruel in a siege of anger. Anger is blind. "Man's anger does not bear the fruit that is acceptable to God."

It is nothing but a violent self-seeking; it shows not the slightest intention of correcting and helping others, but only drunkenness, feverishness, that leads to suffering and destruction.

In this regard, we must beware of that indignation that is often called virtuous when it is aimed at the sins of others. It is almost always something easy, a little hypocritical, and valueless. It calms our nerves, but does no good, especially (and this is usually the case) when one is indignant with those who are not around.

Finally, anger is a lack of respect for God and His providence. Actually, the people on whom we pour out our anger are God's creatures and children, entrusted to our love. Instead of helping men grow and develop, we tend to destroy and annihilate them by our anger.

If we take a closer look, we will see that anger is at heart a revolt against the obstacles and sorrows of life. It is a refusal to consent to what really *is,* an implicit thwarting of God's will for us. We secretly dream of a world that is free from obstacles, from struggles and suffering. But this is not the *real* world. The world in which we live *is* one of trials.

We are within our rights in trying to discover just why this is so. Perhaps the reason is to be found by reflecting on man's liberty, the present imperfection of his being: that of a spirit locked in matter and in time and bogged down by original sin and unbridled desires.

But real understanding will come only after acceptance. And acceptance does not mean slothful resignation.

"To accept suffering, sorrow, and sickness is not to be pleased with them, nor to be a fatalist about them, nor to become hard-headed about them, to benumb ourselves with distraction, nor to try to forget in time. It is, however, offering them to God so that He will make them bear fruit. All this is not a matter for reason, for hypothesis, or understanding; it is a spiritual experience."

We will never understand until we begin to accept. "It's hard to appreciate the savor and food value of something we've never eaten, simply by looking at it."

Let no one say the ideal is too high for most men to strive after. There is no salvation any other way. If men do not consent to *necessity,* it will destroy them. If they do consent, especially if they lovingly consent to *what is,* be it fortune or hardship, *what is* will perfect and elevate them. "For those who love God all things work together unto good." Everything becomes a messenger of God.

". . . in order that a new sense should be formed in us which enables us to hear the universe as the vibration of the word of God, the transforming power of suffering and of joy are equally indispensable. When either of them comes to us, we have to open the very center of our soul to it, just as a woman opens her doors to messengers from her loved one. What does it matter to a lover if the messenger be polite or rough, so long as he gives her a message?"[1]

And so, by continually working for a better world, we must see in those things and events that oppose us the chisel of the Great Sculptor. Getting angry at people or at anything hinders our work, keeps us from fulfilling our mission, and turns the very things meant to help us develop into weapons against us.

[1] Simone Weil, *Waiting for God.*

19. *Patience and Its Seven Secrets*

"Charity is patient," wrote St. Paul. "Blessed are the meek; blessed are the peacemakers," Jesus said. And St. Thomas states that "patience is the virtue of the saints." And St. Francis: "Perfect joy is born of patience."

Truly a Christian virtue—yet how often abused today! "We want action," men will say. "Patience is a passive virture." *Agere est romanum, pati christianum.*[1] This is false, for action is just as Christian as suffering. They are two complementary aspects of life which must be coordinated.

Men look for strength and firmness. But these words, too, can have a Christian meaning. Yet we often give them a strictly pagan sense. "Be tough!" is a motto full of ambiguity. Christ said: "Blessed are the meek."

We can hardly become patient without embodying in ourselves diverse orientations and deep convictions. We are going to point out these secrets of patience and analyze them briefly.

1. *Have convictions!*

We must convince ourselves that few things in the world will make us more pleasing to God, allow us to make more

[1] Action is for Romans; suffering, for Christians.

people happier here below, or give us more interior joy than patience.

Christ Himself assures us of this. Three of the eight beatitudes are devoted to this virtue. It is to the patient and the meek that He promises: "They shall possess the earth."

The violent who do not overcome their violence become dominated by it. They become pure agitators who spread trouble wherever they go. We see them ravaging the world; yet their victory is but an outward one. They win men over, subject, and dominate them, but are never loved by them. At times they become master of man by cleverly swaying his instincts. But they will never win him over by allowing his liberty free play. They rule by fear and dread; and so well do they realize this that they themselves live in constant fear. This is why they periodically weed out others by bloody purges—the instinctive defense of all tyrants!

Only the gentle carry out the work of reconciliation, of union, and of peace. Real bridge-builders! Creative forces of cohesion and unity in the world!

2. *Stay close to God!*

When God becomes the center of our life, things here below take on their proper dimension, one that is small. Readers of *El Cid* know the effect produced on old Diego by a box on the ear. He is beside himself, seized with anger. He feverishly seeks his son to help him revenge himself. Don Diego is no saint. He is a knight filled with the prejudices of his world of "honor." A true man of God would stay calm under such an outrage.

A soul that lives habitually in God's presence does not have to seek God for long if he is wounded or hurt. God is there, living within him. At once the soul echoes the words of the psalmist: "It is good for me, O Lord, that Thou hast humiliated me." And if his heart remains troubled, he repeats this as often as necessary, or falls on his knees until the tempest has passed.

3. *Be humble!*

If someone offends us, let us not say: "What nerve! How dare he outrage *me!*" Rather let us say: "After all, what am I? Nothing much."

Father Zundel recounts how he had to live for years in the immediate vicinity of a fellow who was noise personified. "His presence was enough to ruin silence. He could not speak without being heard in the whole house: his very prayer disturbed the recollection of others . . . his sincerity had the air of absolute certitude. . . ." The priest knew the man did not mean the slightest harm, but this did not stop him from being unbearable. One morning, he had taken just about all he could stand: "I was just about at the limits of my patience with indignation, and could see no way out, when suddenly this question came to my mind: Who are you to be defending yourself with severity, telling the whole world about the outrages you think you're suffering— building up a defense against this onslaught about to over- run you? The answer was as simple as it was evident: there was nothing at all. I stared at the ridiculous and altogether tragic abyss that destroys all that fall within . . . my exaspera- tion and suffering had disappeared. When one is thus dis- tressed, little things lose all proportion. I breathed deeply: I saw clearly now."

4. *Keep still!*

It takes extreme self-control to keep our words cool and serene at a time when we feel wounded to the deepest fibres of our personality. Generally our tone changes, rises, and becomes more and more aggressive in spite of our first resolution to keep calm, and we end up by saying absurd things, so exaggerated that, once we are back to normal again, we are filled with shame. At a time like this, silence is really golden.

Monica, the mother of St. Augustine, presents a good example of patience. We know her husband, Patricius, was no model of gentleness. But, as Augustine tells us, she resisted neither by her actions nor by her words, and always waited until the storm was over to delicately give him a few words of explanation and even some tender reproaches which were almost always well-received. When her friends, bruised and dishonored by the violence of their husbands, complained to her and asked her secret, knowing her husband was very prone to anger, she replied: "Hold your tongue."

There is also a well-known story about St. Francis de Sales. A certain nobleman of the region, who for some reason had a grudge against him, woke up the whole town one morning with his hounds barking and his horns sounding beneath the saint's window. Then this wild fellow and his followers stormed into the palace and severely injured the bishop. St. Francis said nothing and kept his eyes on the ground.

"But Excellency," they asked after the fanatics had left, "how is it that you did not get angry?"

"I made an agreement with my tongue," the saint replied, "that it should say nothing while my heart was excited."

Dale Carnegie tells us that formerly in the German army a soldier who had been insulted did not have the right to file a complaint until he had first of all slept on his grudge and cooled off. If he filed his complaint immediately, he was punished.

"By the eternals," he adds, "there ought to be a law like that in civil life too—a law for whining parents and nagging wives and scolding employers and the whole obnoxious parade of fault-finders."[2]

5. Look ahead!

Most of us in our lives have duties or contacts with others that especially try our patience. Every teacher, for instance, goes through such an ordeal in giving oral examinations, especially when there are many students to examine. We understand only too well the tension that builds up in those who have to ask the same questions on the same subject thirty times a day, and get the same answers, often enough wrong ones. But how much stronger and more justifiable the student's tension must be! For him, the fate of a year of his existence hangs by a thread during that half hour. Moreover, it is astounding to find men of high intellectual formation (and of equally high moral formation, we rightfully suppose, since they are chosen to instruct and educate youth) showing by their uncontrolled annoyance how little mastery they have over themselves.

Would it not be more in conformity with the rules of common courtesy and dignity to welcome the student as a gentleman, to be cordial, and to create the most favorable psychological conditions for a successful result from the test?

Some people, more than others, have the knack of trying our patience. The list of them is striking.

[2] *How to Win Friends and Influence People.*

First of all there are the *bores,* who always turn up at the wrong time, just when one is in a hurry, and who insist in hanging on.

There are the *time-wasters,* who devour time and never know when to leave. They will chatter on for two hours about trivials before getting to the point for which they came in the first place.

There are the *windbags,* who carry on endless monologues to expose their philosophic or political systems to you. You tell them: "I ought to be leaving," and they go with you, accompanying you to your own door.

There are *those who chatter about nothing.* We often bump into them on the train. They steal the peace you hoped for by rambling on about the weather, the passing countryside, or the stations through which you are passing.

There are *those with a one-track mind,* who, after five minutes of conversation, are invariably off on their favorite subject, without asking you if you are at all interested in it.

There are the *busybodies,* bearing sensational news which they alone know and obtained from a reliable source.

There are *sullen spirits, bitter, rebellious, blunt, sceptic, detracting, resentful,* and *base.* Each of them, of course, needs a different treatment. But our patience should not be thwarted by any. How can we infuse a little light, courage, and goodness into each of them?

Then let us humbly call to mind that *we* too . . . !

6. *Apologize!*

Impatience often makes us fall into error. We accuse others of sins and mistakes they have not really committed. When we notice it, it is common courtesy to apologize, even to our inferiors. Let us not think for a moment that we lower ourselves by doing so; on the contrary, we increase, we create confidence, and make ourselves lovable. If we do not apologize, these people will not understand our injustice, whereas if we do ask their pardon, they will easily forgive our anger and our mistakes.

7. Don't be dramatic!

Most quarrels have at their source a trifle which was dramatized.

A spark becomes a conflagration.

A drop of water becomes a flood.

A simple difference of opinion becomes a violent conflict. And all this, just because one has exaggerated something that should really be brought down to its proper proportions.

Quarreling is part and parcel of some families, because everything takes on dramatic proportions: a door banged, a fork in the wrong place, coffee too hot or too cold, potatoes without salt or salted twice, something tipped over, a five minutes' delay, an insignificant over-sight, a trivial clumsiness. Everything in such a family becomes the subject of rebuke and bickering.

Someone once noted in his diary the number of domestic quarrels during his fifteen years of married life, giving the motives for all these squabbles.

Here is a list of the quarrels:

1689 because the table wasn't set right.

1282 because *he* spent too much at the club.

1631 because *she* spent too much at the dressmaker's.

3 because *she* was jealous.

853 because *he* came in with muddy shoes.

550 because *he* didn't want to believe they would both die on the same day.

1 because *she* used an old razor to cut up old clothes.

It would certainly be interesting if each family drew up such a list at the end of each week and examined the causes that bring on the storms. We would then see the trifles that brought on the moans, cries, bitter reproaches, that disturbed for hours on end the serenity of the home.

One member of a committee studied thousands of cases of family breakups. She declared that men leave home especially when they are sick of quarreling with their wives.

But this does not mean that just women have the mania for being dramatic. Some men do the same thing. But women are more exposed to the danger because they are more sensitive to details than men. Living usually in an atmosphere more restrained than men, they tend to give importance to things which are of little importance, compared with the abundance and complexity of affairs in the social and political life.

At any rate, men and women should often repeat to themselves: "It's not *that* important . . . it's so little, it's not even worth the trouble."

20. *Called to Heroism*

THERE is need for courage in all love.

To keep a profound contact with another person, we must conquer our own egotism, put ourselves in the background, purify and renounce ourselves, and become as a simple glance that reaches the other in the intimacy of his personality. This demands a constant effort.

We must also accept his limitations, his powerlessness to become what we would like him to be, his differences, awkwardness, and faults. We simply must accept that he is what he is, all the while longing to see him as he ought to be. This, too, demands much patience. A man's maturing is a slow and unending thing. There are ineradicable manias and natural defects whose havoc we can only diminish, but which we can never wholly root out of those we love. They have ideas with which we shall never agree, and there are areas of their personality which will always remain unknown to us.

As Marie Noël so well put it: "Love is not a day's work."

It takes even more courage to love when the differences between people spring from their very nature. There are people who, united for life, find out too late that they are of an extremely different make-up: the one very refined, the other much too crude. They do not live on the same level. Their interest lies in values of a very different sort. During their courtship, the gap between their two natures was not so noticeable. Youth is a deceiving love potion. With this drink one sees Helen of Troy in every woman and Apollo in every man. But life together soon reveals the initial mistake. Then a very hard trial is imposed on love. The one must not discourage the other by dragging him heartlessly to a system of higher values. The other must not aggravate his inferiority complex, but must open up to him a world which was previously a total stranger to him.

Even when their make-up is more harmonious, it can happen that life together can become very irksome because of the mediocrity of one partner: his indifference, coldness, or thoughtlessness; his lack of sincerity or his demands, his egotism, his never-ending reproaches, his nervous irritability and his complaints, his absolutism and touchiness, his "view-iness" and pettiness, his agressiveness and resentment, or some other fault he has not yet overcome.

If you want to keep love from dying, you must go deep down into yourself; and if you do not go to God, how can love survive?

Finally, there are cases where your charity is really put to a heroic test. This happens especially when one has to live with people who are really bad at heart, or who are psychopaths or sadists who sometimes take fiendish pleasure in making another suffer and who have completely closed their heart to everyone.

And we know that, do what we may, our every advance will be thwarted, our kindness ill-received, and every benevolent word taken as ironical. Even our most insignificant act will be checked by his "What kind of a trap is he laying for me now?"

We feel then that everything is useless, that the love we lavish upon him is worth absolutely nothing. Yes, this is the time for heroism! The hour for real generosity! This is when we must constantly look to God and place all our confidence in Him alone.

The temptation is strong here to try to escape by taking refuge in an ivory tower, or even to return gall for gall, insult for insult, perhaps even blow for blow.

Yet this is the opportunity to prove the exceptional quality of our soul by staying meek, humble, cool, collected. Doubtlessly, it is also an occasion God offers certain souls to prove the full measure of their love.

Jacqueline Vincent, in *L'enfant qui passe,* describes an instance of this staunch fidelity with tragic beauty. It is the story of a woman whose husband's morbid egotism is daily mounting towards a crisis, and whose scorn, rudeness, and foolish demands make a real martyr of his wife. Yet she heroically stays faithful to her home.

When this book first appeared, I was repeatedly asked: "Must one go that far?"

I had to reply: "Unless our nerves give way and we become a burden to the other, unless the welfare of the children demands a change, we *must* stay. This is the time to realize the Epistle of Marriage, to deliver yourself to death for your spouse as Christ did for His Church. Where is it written that our life can never be wholly engaged in a way so sorrowful that moral heroism seems to be the only possible solution?"

The courageous choice of this solution is not found in fiction alone. Here is a touching and real-life testimony. It is the account of a young woman, deceived by the first flutter of her heart, who offers her life to an elegant and good-looking man. He admits he has no deep religious convictions, but promises never to neglect any of his Christian duties. But as soon as they are married, he turns out to be a perfect cynic for whom marriage was just one last fling. His wife tries (although at times a bit awkwardly) to preserve some sort of a religious life in him, but he fails in all his duties and makes her life an agony, a hell on earth. Here are some extracts from her diary:

". . . I wanted him to pray with me in the evening, but he called it foolishness. From then on I prayed alone to God with hidden tears. . . .

"I am constantly seeking in this man to whom I am forever united, a tiny crevice through which I can make my tenderness felt. I seek with growing anguish; a search worse than death; looking forward to the day when I will stop seeking. . . .

". . . My task: to keep this nominal Christian among his brethren in obedience to the Church. At Mass on Sunday, he muttered words of protest, impatience, and mockery against the Church. I pray only with my suffering. . . .

". . . Easter confession and communion were put off for two years. This filled my soul with uneasiness. I won him over only at the price of nearly blasphemous remarks which caused me great distress. The next Easter I again brought up the subject. This time there was an extremely violent scene lasting the whole night, while he berated my 'religious folly' and my art of torturing him. I ended by saying tenderly: 'Am I in the wrong for having taken you at your word? Do you reproach me for it?' He shrugged his shoulders: 'You certainly were foolish to believe it. Everybody knows that promises are made but not kept.'

"The child did not come. I prayed, and pleaded in vain

to see the fulfillment of the motherly instinct that was so
strong in me. God? Yes, God above all. Yet in spite of myself, my hands seek a tangible reality to embrace, mould, and
re-create. I tremble when I meet another lonely heart who
can sense the inexorable appeal of my silence. . . .

"Years have gone by!

"There is no longer any friction between us, for all contact is gone. My God, You know well enough how I wished
with all my heart to make him happy. No, I was never
austere or cold. I know how gay I seemed when I went to
the music hall with him on Christmas day, but deep in my
heart I heard the *Adeste Fideles* in Church, while the
rowdy songstress went through her routine.

". . . I know the sacrament of matrimony gives the
necessary grace to bear this life. Yet its grace does not take
away the suffering. Life grows dull just the same, and one
feels the routine, the futility that accompanies a giving of
self solely out of duty. The way is clear to every temptation—
all, even suicide. Suicide for a Christian, that last resort that
is inconceivable except during a time of pain and disgrace,
so great that the pen refuses to put it down on paper. . . .

". . . There is no doubt, my husband is sick—the doctor's
visits confirm it, but I am kept in the dark. For months I
have sensed the stealthy evolution without being able to
name it. What difference does the name make anyway? I
know the fatal issue is close at hand. My smile is empty; I am
worn out, completely transparent. One would say that he
and I were running a race to the grave. I follow the one I
love purely supernaturally. 'Tell me, dear, do you ever wonder if there is something else in life besides good living and
all the rest?' With a weary gesture, he answers: 'How often
must I tell you I have no soul? And if you could prove to me

that I had one, I would reply that I don't care. . . . Besides, I'd rather be a dog!'

". . . Now he avoids me because his physical failing humiliates him. It is a secret drama which I penetrate with inexpressible pity. Having lived wrapt in self-love—to end it prematurely with such senility, such rapid decomposition of the flesh, to draw closer to that grave each day!

". . . For the last two years my sleep was broken several times a week by outcries and blasphemies. My husband was speaking to God as to a visible enemy, spewing his rancor, and insulting Him in the vilest ways.

". . . Then I would slip to the floor and pray with out-stretched arms; I placed the weight of my love on the other side of the scales. I know that such crimes are slight, since they come from an almost unconscious heart. But they hurt me just the same; my face is seeped in sweat and tears. I seem to live in a state of endless agony. . . .

"One grey winter's day, he locked me in his wasted arms, and rested his livid cheek on my breast, giving me the most moving testimony possible: 'You have been an angel in my life.' I knew it was not true, but finding him suddenly accessible, I stroked his brow, disregarding the protests that rose within me and I spoke to him like a mother of the great peace that a priest could bring in these trying hours. He accepted on principle to receive him before dying, to conform to family 'tradition.' 'Only,' he added, '*I* will be the judge of the right moment. Neither you nor the doctor will have a thing to say.' But this moment of clarity was his last.

"One night, I found him dead. He had died all alone, without God and without tenderness.

"Alone with his yet warm body, I told him all he had

refused to hear in those twenty years: words of love, of suffering, foolish words; all I had passionately wanted, all I had missed so miserably. He had not been able to glimpse that magnificent happiness that rises from heaven to earth. And I had never lived an hour of it. The sad shepherdess, made sterile instead of being a mother, could not lead him whom she had taken so boldly under her care. I wanted to do great things, but everything was doomed to failure. . . . And yet, though he drank occasionally, he never became a drunkard; though he sought pleasure, he never became depraved: I stripped this violent man of as many pretexts to insult God as I could.

"And that is all."

That is all, at least apparently. But who would not believe that such a love must have saved him, even if he did not show a visible sign of conversion?

As for her, having accepted the trial, she found peace. "Every soul that is tried is awaited by God at heaven's gate. To step through it, the password is indispensable: it is the *fiat* of love. . . .

"God's intentions often remain mysterious to us here below. But He pities the poor who adhere to Him without understanding, in a spirit of faith and love. And then, He gives them His peace and His joy.

"The soul is at peace. These physiological and psychological reactions are not just the peace and calm after the storm. The soul is lifted up and with a growing intensity sees what was dead and destroyed radiantly revivified under a heaven that grows ever closer. The words so close to men: 'happiness and wretchedness,' 'success and failure' lose all value and force in this truth: there is but one destiny: eternity. Everything is made clear and is amplified; in losing its finitude, everything returns to its source. The soul is but a spark consumed with a dazzling certitude: it will return to the eternal Hearth from which it came.

"Nothing else has any importance."

21. *The Infernal Circles*

PROPERLY understood, charity is "an ascent to heaven." It is the light, freedom, communion, the very outpouring and radiation of oneself. It is a participation in God's providence, His creative power, and His intimate joy. It is the "possession of the world," an anticipation and foretaste of heaven.

On the other hand, everything contrary to charity is a descent into hell. We are going to follow, in this chapter, one by one the infernal circles which drag so many down to their own loss and woe.

Rare indeed are those of us who have not set foot on this dark staircase—perhaps unwittingly! And that is the most dangerous part of all! For who knows just how far we may go down if one day the evil forces dormant in our hearts explode at the shock of a serious injury or undeserved suffering?

1. *Egoism.*

The first circle is egoism.

Katherine Mansfield writes that people today are perverted by too much self-interest: what happens to *me;* look at *me;* look what happened to *me.* It is like trying to run, she says, while a huge black snake wraps itself around you.

Egoism fetters us to ourselves. It makes us more and more closed in, incomprehensible, inaccessible, and hostile.

It takes on a thousand forms.

There is the naive egoism of the child who candidly shows off his ego: "Look at *my* pretty dress . . . look at *my* beautiful doll."

We find it among grown-ups too. Everyone who takes a good look at himself easily discerns the tendency to talk about himself, what *he* has done, what *he* knows, about the situations where *he* came out on top. An experiment carried on in New York showed that the words most employed in telephone conversations were the little word "I" and its twin brother "me." And we all know that in the snapshot of a group, we instinctively look for ourself first.

A more serious, and not at all rare, type of egoism is found among those who are so concerned with their own comfort and ease, their own interests, that they accuse others of egoism as soon as they are asked to make a slight sacrifice for the welfare of their neighbor.

This kind of egoism made a humorist say: "Egoism is like stoutness. The more you have of it, the more another's gets in your way."

Here is a striking example of this kind of egoism: "A young lad of eighteen was just about recovering from a very acute case of pneumonia. His very busy father could only visit his son's room a few times a day. It was his idea to come in with a lighted cigar and have his coffee in the sick boy's room. In a few moments smoke clouded the room. The father ought to have forseen the result: the sick boy was seized with a violent fit of coughing.

" 'I'm sorry to bother you,' he said to his father, 'but I don't think I can stand the smoke any longer.'

" 'You've become very soft and difficult during this illness, my boy,' the father replied. 'If the smoke bothers you, good night! You know that I can't get along without my cigar!' "

There is yet another morbid egoism, so implanted in the heart that it eats it away like a cancer. It is that of the man who not only loves himself alone, but also frightens all about him into the service of his ego. Although people hasten to satisfy him, he feels forgotten and abandoned—even wronged and persecuted. If someone resists his whims at all, he complains he is tortured. And when one yields to his fancies, he begins to pretend he is being made fun of.

There is finally an egoism that is . . . I was going to say heroic, but let us rather say . . . diabolic. It is a veritable intoxication with self, affirming its self-sufficiency and setting up against God. It is that of Nietzsche, who wished "the death of God"; it is that of Jaurès, for whom "God is an equal with whom one argues, not the master before whom one bows"; it is that of Jacques Rivière, who said before his conversion: "I will always have myself." And many others follow suit.

Egoism is the cancer of personality. It believes it feeds itself by reducing everything to self. But it only feeds upon evil. It only works toward its own destruction.

2. *Sadness at the sight of good.*

We also find in many a vague and profound sadness over what is good. It is not quite envy, however, but rather a type of mild inner spite at the sight of the "good luck" other people have.

"In the unhappiness that befalls our friends there is something that does not displease us."

St. Paul said that charity rejoices over good. The only "protection" we have from the good fortune of others is love. Every time we see happiness enter the home of another, we ought to pray: "Be praised, O Lord, for the happiness You are giving my brother. I rejoice with him over it. And more to his happiness, O wondrous God."

Then, we will be like the elect: Dante tells us that when a new soul arrives in heaven, the radiant souls run toward him, crying out with joy: "Lo! one who shall increase our love!"

3. Envy and jealousy.

History is made up, for the most part, of tragedies brought about by envy. From the dawn of the world, it made its appearance with the devil, who could not stand God's superiority: "I will not serve; I will be like the Most High." Cast far from God because of his rebellion, he could not stand seeing Adam and Eve happy, and led them into his own ruin—by provoking what sentiment? Envy: "What is this talk of death? God knows well that as soon as you eat this fruit your eyes will be opened, and you yourselves will be like gods, knowing good and evil."

The first crime was a crime committed out of envy: Cain murdered his brother Abel. And since then, almost all crimes have sprung from envy. Most quarrels, revolutions, and wars have no other origin.

Envy consists in being sad over the goods of others which we ourselves do not have.

Jealousy is rather the fear that others will get hold of what we possess. It is a love that is at once exclusive, uneasy, monopolizing, possessive, and egoistic. It is quite a complicated affair, and in certain situations (for example, conjugal love, whose very essence is to be exclusive) jealousy, within limits, is perhaps a legitimate part of affection and has no displeasing aspect to it. But it quickly degenerates and, like its cousin envy, becomes a sentiment that is fierce, tormented, sullen, and dissolvent.

Jealousy and envy extend to everything: affection, riches, beauty, talent, power, honor, and happiness. No form of good or superiority escapes them.

In many instances, they are real sicknesses. Some people suffer from them as from an incurable disease. As long as they disown them, do not willingly give in, and turn a deaf ear to their suggestions, we must look upon these unfortunate men as victims and not as blameworthy.

But woe to those who yield to these dangerous instincts. No act is too perverse for them to commit. The envious sometimes use open warfare, sometimes concealed attack. By mockery and even rude insults they do their best publicly to humiliate their victims. At other times they slyly put on a disguise and act through insinuations. Sometimes they underhandedly busy themselves with such things as anonymous letters or other devilish schemes to lay heavy suspicion on the character of the people they envy.

Dante, in his *Purgatorio,* condemns envious souls to a terrible punishment: "all their eyelids an iron wire pierces and stitches up . . ." and they, "through the horrible seam, were pressing forth tears so that they bathed their cheeks." Why the eyes? Because they did not know how to look with joy upon the happiness of others. Let them be condemned, then, no longer to see anything during their punishment.

4. *Resentment.*

Sadness at the sight of good, envy, and spite often join forces to make up that explosive substance called "resentment."

It consists in a basic hostility toward an ensemble of values in which one neither can nor wishes to take part, although he looks at them with nostalgia. It is basically the story of the fox and the grapes, but it is an infinitely more somber and tragic tale.

We see as many examples of it in private life as we do in social life. Think of the resentment that tears at the hearts of those who have met disgrace, of certain old spinsters and bachelors, or some social classes, of all apostates.

It happens that life, and sometimes their own fault, has made them unappreciative of certain values such as beauty, marriage, youth, culture, and faith. Not being able to claim these, they discredit them, falsify them, and block them out of their mind. Beauty is only vanity; marriage is but a lowly quest for sensual satisfaction or simply a prison; youth is but a time of folly and ridicule; intellectual and moral culture is only snobbery, affectation, and sham; faith is only a hodgepodge of absurdities.

"They are too green," said the fox. Nevertheless, resentful men keep an attachment for these values that is as violent as it is powerless, and here lies the woeful and tormenting inner contradiction. They know well that they are insidiously deceiving themselves and are substituting a lost paradise with their rancor.

From the values themselves, their resentment naturally turns toward those who appreciate and enjoy them. It is in such people that they seek to extinguish these values, disparage and destroy them. Think, for instance, of class hatred. Or think of a Nietzsche and his attacks upon Christians—of a Nietzsche who sees only impotence in goodness, craven baseness in humility, cowardice in obedience. Think of the violent attacks of some apostates against their former faith.

5. *Hate.*

Resentment leads directly to hatred. Whereas love is a creative force, hate is a destructive, annihilating power. One day I read a frightful article in a newspaper. It was an apology of hatred, full of a sophistry that had the air of hell itself.

Rarely have I read a page that was more contradictory to the Gospel. It said, for example: "Hate is much more fruitful than love." And to ridicule the latter, the writer added: "Hatred gains battles; love founds humane societies for animals." Then he continued: "Hatred and scorn lead to heroism more directly than love . . . to take away from man his warlike instincts is to kill humanity."

Everybody can see easily enough what type of ideology inspired such falsehoods. They remind me of a page written twenty years earlier by the Soviet Commissar Lounatcharsky: "We hate Christianity and Christians; even the best among them ought to be considered as our worst enemies. They preach love of neighbor and mercy, which are contrary to our principles. Christian love is a fetter to the development of the revolution. Down with love of neighbor! We must know how to hate; only at this price will we conquer the universe."

Hate! Nothing ravages a man's conscience and soul more than hate.

Love, tenderness, true charity flood man with light, joyously enveloping his whole person, shining forth with resplendency. Hate, on the contrary, darkens the soul in a night that envelops and swallows it up. Instinctively when we speak of hate we think of darkness.

It is also like a poison flowing through our veins that destroys us. Resentment, says Max Scheler, is a "psychological self-poisoning."

Hatred is suffering to which one morbidly clings. Naturally, in speaking of envy, resentment, and hate, we associate them with what is diabolic and hellish. Nothing so suits the devil as these sentiments. In Milton's *Paradise Lost,* Satan thus explains the essence of his being: "All good for me is lost; evil, be thou my good!" But, heaven always forces its light into his soul, and he is forced to gaze at heaven, which stirs up all the more the infernal fire in his heart: for the more he sees of the great joy there, the more he feels the torment within him . . . every good becomes suffering for him. So it is with the man who is resentful and who hates.

Now, who of us has not, at certain moments of his life, felt bitterness, violence, and hate enkindle and rise up in him? It was about to engulf everything. . . . We had to hold down our heart for long periods and fall on our knees before Him who was the Victim of hatred, and pray . . . pray . . . with Him, "Forgive them . . ." until we were calm again.

Ah, what an error it is to pretend, as the article cited above, that "hate is difficult to learn," that it supposes, not only a strange firmness and a will that is ever tense, but that it demands still an unceasing self-conquest, that one does not arrive at hatred over night, but must undergo a series of inner victories over self—that hate is a gift only to those who can merit it, whereas love is within everybody's reach.

One who speaks like that must have never fathomed his own heart. In order to hate, it is enough to yield to the instincts that sleep within us, which the slightest shock can awaken. All we have to do is to give in to the dark and evil powers which only ask to be let free to engulf us.

It is *love* that is a conquest; it is love that demands an incessant struggle to rise above the forces of egoism that hold us perpetually immersed in ourselves. Love is a hard victory.

It is love that is fruitful. Hatred smashes and dismembers everything: families, regions, countries, the world. If the world has become a bloody jungle where men kill each other, it is because egoism, greed, covetousness, and hatred have spoken forth louder than love.

Maritain wrote twenty-five years ago, "Only a deluge of charity can save the world." We have not had that deluge of charity. We have had a deluge of blood.

Christianity is love. Even when it wills the punishment of sin (and it does so with all its might), it is not with a spirit of vengeance, but in hope of bringing back the sinner to the harbor of love.

"My little children," said St. John, "let us love one another, for love springs from God; no one can love without being born of God and knowing God. How can the man who has no love have any knowledge of God, since God is love?"

22. *Be Courteous*

IT'S A curious thing, but we never hear a woman being referred to as "courteous." We may hear that she is obliging, affable, or kind, but never courteous.

Courtesy seems to be a man's virtue. Perhaps the qualities that go to make it up are so innate in woman that it is superfluous and almost unnecessary to speak of them as far as she is concerned. It may be that so few men pay attention to the little virtues it demands: attention, politeness, refinement, and affability. Whatever the case may be, if courtesy is man's privilege, it must be admitted that he uses it sparingly. Men who are courteous to all without exception are rare. And this state of affairs does not add to humanity's happiness.

Courtesy is a virtue that has a common air about it. It is expressed by a host of gestures, none of which are spectacular; yet the ensemble reveals an attentive spirit to those who observe a heart that is forgetful of self, and a goodness that is ever alert. It puts harmony and charm in the ordinary hum-drum of life. It is a discreet and humble virtue that especially avoids omissions and offenses:

—not slamming doors, or walking heavily when we enter a house where people are already sleeping;

—not playing the radio too loudly with all the windows

open, when there is someone sick in the neighborhood who needs quiet, or a family in mourning, or simply a student anxiously preparing for an impending examination;

—not hurrying or jostling others to get the best place in a streetcar, bus, or train;

—not blurting out that witty joke or remark that will offend;

—not letting our clothes or other objects lie around, so that our wife, sister, mother, or maid will have to put them in their place;

—not letting our cigarette ashes fall outside the ashtray;

—not coming in with muddy shoes, which will only increase the work of those who care for the upkeep of the house;

—not ironically and harshly calling attention to some involuntary blunder: a broken glass, a tipped-over vase, a burnt dish, a forgotten promise.

This is all of little importance. Someone has said that courtesy is not a virtue that "pays dividends." It betters, dispenses joy, and lets air and sunshine into our dark and weary world. Where it is missing, the sky is grey, gloomy, and desolate.

Many men look down on these little virtues. Certain others see only mannerisms in them, affectations, effeminacy. Of course, courtesy may become warped, as can any virtue. It can lack simplicity and even truth. For this reason it is better to have every action firmly rooted in sincere charity. Many men, and especially young men, scorn every form of politeness as if it were hypocritical. They confuse frankness with bluntness and crudeness.

"The spirit of truth ought to be understood in connexion with charity which is the 'sun of the virtues.' Charity should always be present; it should color every other virtue. Just because we champion the truth, we do not have to speak with insolence and rudeness; nor do we need to speak with cutting words."

In such instances, the spirit of truth becomes petty and even cynical. A cynic loves to throw around inopportune truths. He speaks the truth, not because it is true, but because, in the present circumstances and in the way in which he says it, it is shocking, indecent, and cutting.

As to pettiness, it is a left-over from barbarism, and it drives some men to all kinds of improprieties, either unwittingly, boastfully, or sadistically. In some, however, it is present under the form of passing urges, caused by fatigue or nervousness. These people make humiliating observations about their wife in the presence of a third party; they slap and yell at their children; they are overbearing with their inferiors. But note how kind and generous they can be at other times. They are not always heartless, but at these moments they lose their head. These men who in their daily life know how to be charming and distinguished now give in to violent words and actions.

For others the lack of kindness is often chronic. It follows them everywhere. They are horrible men who display a free and easy behavior in a despicable manner, with insulting and cutting remarks. They are coarse, vulgar, and base people whose company is always odious and, at times, a martyrdom.

The deplorable thing about it (something obvious to everyone) is that these people believe they are dispensed from the laws of common courtesy especially toward those closest to them. Everyone knows that at home people feel freed from many constraints. The man who had to "put on an act" or "turn on the charm" in his public life, can at last relax. Actually, this is one of the great advantages of the family: one feels at ease. But does it not happen that we relax a little too much at times, to the detriment of the other members of the family, and the whole family spirit?

"It is an amazing but true thing that practically the only people who ever say mean, insulting, wounding things to us are those of our own households. . . . No woman can ever understand why a man doesn't put forth the same effort to make his home a growing concern as he does to make his business or profession a success.

"But, although to have a contented wife and a peaceful and happy home means more to a man than to make a million dollars, not one man in a hundred ever gives any real serious thought or makes any honest effort to make his marriage a success. He leaves the most important thing in his life to chance, and he wins out or loses, according to whether fortune is with him or not. Women can never understand why their husbands refuse to handle them diplomatically when it would be money in their pockets to use the velvet glove instead of the strong-arm method."[1]

But is it a question of diplomacy and interest here? By no means! It is not in egotistical motives that courtesy should seek its nourishment, but rather in respect and love, and in the desire to make someone happy and to create something worth while.

---

[1] Dale Carnegie, *How to Win Friends and Influence People.*

23. *In Judging We Are Judged*

At first, we are surprised at the severity with which Christ forbids us to judge others. And why not! Are there not men whose faithlessness, hypocrisy and wickedness are as plain as day? Is not shutting our eyes the same as denying what is evident? And to abstain from speaking—isn't that one of the ways of becoming an accomplice in another's crime?

"Judge not," says Christ. And the motive He gives is very striking. Your judgment is going to fall on your own head; it is going to reveal the hidden sentiments of your own heart; as we would say today, it is going to psycho-analyze you. "For with the judgment you judge, you shall be judged," said our Saviour. If only this revelation of our subconscious could somehow be useful in correcting our secret faults! But is has absolutely no value since we reveal ourselves only to *others* in our judgments. Rather they darken the obscurity which already surrounds us. They turn our eyes from our own defects and focus them only on the faults of others.

What our judgments reveal in us, first of all, is a more or less accentuated tendency to resentment. Our reactions to evil, our judgments of evil, our struggles against the evil in others are not exactly innocent. This is perhaps one of the most dangerous powers of evil: it can engender evil in others.

"The fight against evil easily acquires an evil character itself; it becomes infected by evil. There is a sinister moral dialectic of Manichaean dualism. Too, great foes of evil become evil themselves. This is a paradox of the conflict with evil and with evil men and things. The good become evil for the sake of victory over evil, and do not believe in the use of other methods than evil in the conflict against evil. Kindliness invites an attitude of disdain; it appears to be uninteresting and insipid. Malice, on the other hand, imposes itself and appears more interesting and more attractive. . . . It is only the Gospel which overcomes this rebirth of the conflict with evil in the form of a new evil, and regards the condemnation of sinners as a new sin. One must behave with humanity and kindliness even to the devil."[1]

"Hitler's greatest crime—an unforgivable thing—was to have dragged all civilization downhill; not so much that he transformed Germany into a huge barracks, trampled upon human dignity, and glorified the most atrocious barbarism— but that he forced other nations to act in the same way to save their life and liberty; that he brought to the surface, among the most civilized and peaceful nations, those strange enemies rooted in the depths of man which centuries of efforts had tried to bury; he let loose primitive hate in the world, love of destruction, and of blood; he built in the twentieth century a 'stone idol with an unalterable smile.' "[2]

Does this mean that we must stop seeing evil, stop denouncing and fighting it? No! But we must begin at home

[1] Nicolas Berdyaev, *The Divine and the Human* (Chicago: Alec R. Allenson, Inc., 1949).

[2] Lecomte du Noüy, *Human Destiny* (New York: Longmans, Green & Company, 1947).

and stay at home. As to the evil in others, we ought to combat it with good, avoiding judgments of another's secret intention and jealously guarding the purity of our own intentions and the means we employ.

Besides, most of the time, the necessary elements to make an honest judgment are not at our disposal. We only see the outside. We only know fragmentary aspects of an act or a person. We ought to repeat to ourselves a hundred times a day, "I just don't know." Actually, what we know the least is our own ignorance.

A second defect that our ill-willed judgments reveal to those who hear us is a certain lack of intelligence and nar- row-mindedness. People will say: "What a skinflint! Al- though he lives in a rich mansion, people knock in vain at his door, and he gives almost nothing to the poor or to charity." What they do not know is that he is up to his neck in debts, that his house is only a front, and that he is on the verge of bankruptcy.

People will say again: "What a stupid chatterbox she is." Perhaps they do not know that she is much smarter than she appears, but that she has a strange inferiority complex. Her words are simply a reaction of self-defense. Besides, she knows it, and suffers very much from it, and continually worries about it.

When one has the occasion, as priests and doctors often do, to penetrate behind the scenes of a soul, he is always surprised to find men very different from their outward appearance. Both better and worse! Every person has his desert regions, and his fertile areas—his pagan lands, and his sanctuary where burns a sacred flame. Even the worst of men! God alone scrutinizes the heart and soul. God alone knows what a creature has done. God alone is judge.

Most of our judgments, therefore, reveal much misunderstanding on our part. Have you ever noticed how the aspect of a moral fault varies as to whether I or another has committed it? There are, for instance, those defensive little lies so many people tell. They are hardly deliberate and are said instinctively, just as one would raise his arm to ward off a blow. When this happens to us, it is an "accident"; and we find a thousand excuses for it. This insincere act is so much a part of our personality that we can look at it objectively only at the price of a considerate criticism of ourselves. But put this lie in another's mouth; and suppose, moreover, that you yourself are the victim. Now everything takes on a different color and you cannot find words severe enough to condemn such conduct.

Why? Because, in others, we see evil apart from the states of conscience that go into its making and growth. We see evil in the raw, without its roots, its background, and all that goes to *explain,* but not *justify,* the sudden eruption.

This could be said of any kind of fault. Even in the gravest faults there are elements that escape us and lessen the guilt a great deal. What is mortal in our eyes may be only venial in the sight of God, who sees all. What is objectively grave can be a slight fault in a particular case.

It suffices to observe ourselves closely to notice how at certain moments of our life we spoke or acted in a way that did not correspond to our real self. Fatigue, lack of attention or reflexion—who can say? Later, when we think back on it, we are surprised and deeply saddened: did I really do that? What have I done? With this in mind, how indulgently ought we to treat others!

Our judgments very often also prove that we completely

lack a critical spirit either with regard to what we are told or with regard to ourselves.

One does not need to be a keen observer to know how much people distort facts. Men are poor observers. It's enough to have been present at an event to know how newspapers distort facts. Just check up on some petty gossip sometime, and you will see the gross errors committed. Frequently we fall for calumnies that have no basis whatsoever.

This ought to sharpen our critical spirit and make us put question marks and "maybe's" on all the unkind remarks made about our neighbor. But instead of this, how childlessly gullible so many people are—taking gossip for sterling silver and spreading it around.

In other cases we lack a critical spirit of ourselves. Some judgments at times show an amazing thoughtlessness. I once heard a manufacturer bitterly criticize Catholics for abandoning the whole film industry to unscrupulous and amoral businessmen. Although he himself was a Catholic (and a rich one), the idea never occurred to him to take the initiative and gather capital to organize a Catholic film industry.

I remember another businessman whom I desired to interest in supporting certain projects. "I have my own work," he replied. And he explained to me that he had founded with his own money several projects rival to those of the parish. After passing everyone through the strainer of his haughty criticism, he showed me to the door and added: "Too bad we don't understand one another better. What good we could do. Didn't Christ Himself say that we ought to be *one?*"

What is to be said for these judgments by which one

casts suspicion on the highest of values, by declaring them impossible and therefore tainted with deceit and hypocrisy.

For some people piety is only bigotry; fervor, humbug; humility, an inferiority complex; pardon, cowardice; generosity, an endeavor to cover over sordid interest; chastity, a lack of temperament or just plain hypocrisy.

"What is base tends to spread itself," said Saint Exupéry —and that is the sad thing we see here: a base soul drags everything down to his own level; he believes in nothing beautiful or pure or gratuitous, nothing in the world that is disinterested.

The deepest reason why we are forbidden to judge and condemn is that by doing so we infallibly reveal a lack of love. One does not condemn those he loves. Not that he is blind to their faults and perhaps the evil in them, but he looks at them long and patiently to understand them better. He sees beyond the evil—he sees them in their personality. He never dreams of standing up as a judge to them. Rather like a father or mother, his only concern is to care for them, heal them, and hope in the triumph of good.

24. A Neighbor to All

Do you know the parable of the Good Samaritan?
Of course!
But, do not be too sure.
"Who is my neighbor?" asked a doctor of the law.
Jesus then told him the story of a poor man left for dead

by robbers. A priest passes by and looks the other way. A Levite passes . . . the same story. Then a Samaritan comes along, and he extends a helping hand. Which of these three men, in your opinion, was a neighbor to him who fell among thieves?

"In this parable, Jesus gives the word 'neighbor' an *active* meaning—one which we do not think of often. 'Who is my neighbor?' asked the scribe. Jesus replied: 'Be a neighbor to everybody'; that is, be the man who is truly helpful, who bends with mercy over the misery of man—every man —the first one who comes along, be he stranger, or even an adversary, as was the Samaritan."

To be interested, to go out to meet a neighbor's needs, not to wait for him to make the first move, like the Blessed Virgin at the wedding feast of Cana—with open eyes, ears attentive; not in order to satisfy our curiosity, but to catch the cares of the world in flight, to sense when and how we can be of use without imposing ourselves, to serve without being in the way—here are some of the most positive signs of true charity.

Charity is giving attention to another; it is respect for, a deep understanding of one's neighbor. But this inner attitude would be vain and deceitful if our charity did not become active and manifest itself in various services for our neighbor's benefit. Charity is a spirit, but one that has hands to be used.

In the light of the Gospel, it seems that we shall be judged primarily on our omissions with regard to our neighbor. "For I was hungry, and you did not give me to eat; I was thirsty and you gave me no drink; I was a stranger and you did not take me in; naked, and you did not clothe me; sick, and in prison, and you did not visit me."

We would like to excuse ourselves: "Lord, when did we see thee hungry, or thirsty, or a stranger, or naked, or sick, or in prison, and did not minister to thee?"

Then Christ will say; "Amen I say to you, as long as you did not do it for one of these least ones, you did not do it for me."

"But we didn't think," we will say. Poor excuse. We should have thought.

There would be a thousand things to say here—many often repeated, but which so often remain absent from our lives. We will point out only a few of them.

First of all, there is group-spirit. By that I mean being ever alert to give those who live with us or whom we meet along the way the helping hand necessary to save them from a slight embarrassment or pay them some small service. To help a traveler board a train, to rearrange your baggage so there is room for his, to offer to carry a package which appears too heavy for him, to stop and help a fellow traveler in distress—these are all opportunities for group-spirit. But how many of us remain blind to these little needs.

An example: on one of the main thoroughfares of a big city, at eight in the morning, a fourteen-year-old lad is pushing a four-wheeled cart loaded with a sack of coal. Suddenly the sack slides forward, the cart takes a nose-dive, and the two back wheels are up in the air. The little fellow tries to pull the cart upright without any success. It is of no use to lean on the back, for as soon as he lets go, the cart goes down again in front. All he needs to do is move the sack back, but to do that he would have to lift it up entirely, for it bulges on all sides and refuses to be moved. The spunky lad tries, but in vain, since he just is not strong enough.

Nine people successively pass by him on the sidewalk—
look at him . . . and keep on going. Not one of them thinks
of giving him the hand he needs. It would not take ten
seconds. Up we go! and the sack is in place, the cart is
balanced, and the little fellow sets out merrily on his way,
with a sparkle in his eyes and a grateful smile on his lips.

We must also say a word about almsgiving. It is not
valued much in our day. We no longer like to hear of it.
Justice ought to take care of all that. It is right, in fact, that
charity first of all obliges us to be just, not only in our private
relations, but equally in our social behavior. Take the case of
the wealthy Peter Girard, who astounded the world with a
last will filled with vast legacies to charitable foundations,
but during his lifetime he had mercilessly ruined thousands
of people. Without going so far as that, some rich people
very often show themselves quite generous in helping the
poor and supporting charities, yet turn a deaf ear to the pressing appeals of the Popes for more social justice. Happily
there are others who know how to harmonize all their
duties.

No matter how great the advance of social organization
is, there is always a vast field that remains open to the initiatives of charity. The Fathers of the Church had some fiery
words on this subject. They have been accused of lacking
discretion.

"The superfluity of the rich is the necessity of the poor;
thus to possess the superfluous is to keep back the good of
others" (St. Augustine).

"The rich kill the poor when they retain the means that
could save them from death" (St. Gregory the Great).

"It is a grave fault for you to leave your neighbor in misery; you know he is deprived of what is necessary, that he

suffers hunger, that he is in need; you know he is ashamed
to admit his distress and yet you do not help him; this is a
great sin" (St. Ambrose).

"When you own more than is necessary for food and
clothing, give what is superfluous to the poor and know that
in doing this you are but a debtor" (St. Jerome).

"The bread which you have left over belongs to the poor;
the clothes you keep needlessly in your room belong to the
naked; the shoes you leave unused belong to those unfortunate people who must go barefoot; you do wrong, therefore,
to the poor whom you could help" (St. Basil).

Pope Leo XIII echoed these glowing texts when he wrote
in his Encyclical *Rerum Novarum*: "But if the question be
asked, 'How must one's possessions be used?'—the Church
replies without hesitation: 'Man should not consider his
outward possessions as his own, but as common to all, so as
to share them without difficulty when others are in need.
This is why the Apostle said: Command the rich of this
world to give easily and to share their riches.' True, no one
is commanded to distribute to others what is necessary for
his own well-being and that of his household; nor even to
give away what is reasonably required to keep up becom-
ingly his condition in life. . . . But when necessity has been
supplied, and one's position fairly considered, it is a duty to
give to the indigent out of that which is over."

I know very well that doubts arise precisely when it is a
question of determining what conveniences are necessary or
what one's position in life demands.

Here each one is obliged to follow his own conscience.
But it would be desirable for this conscience to stay more
constantly on the alert for the needs of the poor. How much,
for example, could we detract from our relaxations in order

How Much Patience Have You?

HOW PATIENT AND LONG-SUFFERING is the Lord! We poor humans are depending on these attributes of God all the time. We disobey His commandments; we expect His forgiveness. He is the God of mercy and justice Who will one day judge us.

In our daily dealings with those about us, how often do we not fail to imitate His patience and long-suffering? Someone answers us sharply or unkindly and we go into a "slow burn." Perhaps we explode and the result is a major fracture of charity—a situation that might continue for years.

Or, we hear a comment that has been made about us by a person who has judged us unjustly. Our first natural reaction is one of anger and indignation. Why should this happen to us?

* * *

THE SON OF GOD, during His 33 years on earth, taught us many lessons and in the gospels we cannot help but be impressed by His patience. He was accused of being a wine-bibbler, an associate of sinners. He was charged with undermining the power of Caesar. He was sneered at as a mere "son of a carpenter."

In the closing hours of His life, He was subjected to a massive amount of false testimony, a brutal scourging, ignominious treatment by the soldiers, and finally, nailed to the cross, to die thereon. Without complaint, with equanimity, with patience He bore these trials and pains.

He was the sinless One, the Son of God. He bore all of this to atone for your sins and mine. We who are sinners deserve much punishment for our sins. When God allows us to be hurt by an unkind word or to be disturbed by an unjust judgment or to be humiliated in one way or another, He is giving us a chance to imitate the patience which Christ has taught us.   —F.J.K.

POPE PAUL noted that this insistence on man's mortality "drives many souls away from the Faith and from the Church, especially the young and the children of our time who want joy, beauty and the enjoyment of life."

He said that instead "Christianity is the religion of the Cross, the Church is the teacher of mortification. All this does not conform to the modern spirit which seeks happiness."

But he went on, it is this insistence on the frailty of life that is "frankly realistic."

He said that "when the Church speaks to us about the briefness of our earthly existence it deals with the most common and most obvious experience of our present condition and it deals with it flatly and bluntly, with the undeniable language of the pessi-

victory of good over evil, of happiness over sorrow, of holiness over sin and of life over death."

Holy See Supports Lay Operated School

BRIDGEPORT, Conn. — (NC) —The Bishop of Bridgeport said here the Sacred Congregation of Seminaries and Universities has backed the lay administration and faculty of new Sacred Heart university.

Bishop Walter W. Curtis made the announcement to the diocese's priests during a yearly progress report meeting about the one-year-old university operated as a commuter, co-educational college. It is headed and staffed entirely by laymen.

Bishop Curtis also said that Pope Paul VI has given his blessing to the university.

to help the needy more generously? Some people make it a rule to give equally as much to the poor as they spend on their own pleasures. That is something to meditate on! Why not make it your rule?

Another question often brought up is this: how much should I limit myself and even deprive myself of in order to be able to give more generously to charity, and practice at the same time our Lord's command to mortify myself?

In every instance, we note this: if many people accept easily enough the restrictions circumstances impose upon them (as during war, when some people were compelled to lead ascetic lives), very few, even among Christians, take the initiative of seriously denying themselves without being forced out of necessity.

Another problem arises especially for professional men such as industrialists, doctors, and lawyers. When one succeeds in his profession and feels his own power developing and reaching its peak, what limit should he voluntarily fix to the amount of his activities, so as to permit others, younger and perhaps less talented or dynamic than he, to take a place in a field which would give them a chance to live, build a home, and raise a family?

Surely this is a problem that implies a good number of elements and whose solution is likewise to be left to each one's conscience. But how often do we see anyone even posing the question? And if so, is it answered generously? It seems, however, that for many men, voluntary restrictions upon their professional activities would not only be a fine act of charity, but would also give them the necessary leisure for their specialized or general culture, for the education of their family, their religious life, and their apostolate.

We do see that the opportunities are not lacking. Charity has a vast field before it, open to its initiatives. It is in multiplying these that men will come closer to each other.

A priest wrote an article several years ago entitled "Re-weaving." He explains there that people are like a cloth. When the threads are locked tightly one to the other, the cloth can catch the wind and power a boat, resist water and air, warm our bodies. Separated, these threads are powerless and useless. Pulled apart, they hardly render any more service.

Suppose, for instance, that American cloth (the American people) were pulled out of shape, even torn. It would have to be re-woven. How? By being careful to miss no occasion for rendering service, and so to re-establish a flow of sympathy and love between men disunited by mistrust, indifference, and hatred.

Is our cloth torn?

We need menders—legions of them.

25. Be There!

THE mystery of someone's presence! It is not always necessary to do or say something to make someone happy or comfort him. Besides, it's not always possible. It is enough to *be there* . . . to be present with all your powers of sympathy and affection.

There is a storm. The children are afraid, and mother is ill at ease. Father is not at home, but suddenly he returns

. . . and calm re-enters their hearts, as if he could defend them from lightning by his presence alone!

Baby is crying upstairs—afraid of a noise, the dark, or a mere trifle. But when his mother appears, a smile immediately wipes away the tears. A warm presence is there, powerful and protective, reassuring and calming, like a god's.

"I am so lonely," cried the newly arrived patient. She no longer had her parents—only a distant cousin, married and mother of a family, whose preoccupations were elsewhere. Here she was unknown, everything was so strange. . . .

How many there are who have no one in their lives, like the paralytic at the pool of Bethsaida who said to Christ: "I have no one . . . no one to help me down into the water at the right moment." But Christ was there . . . and was for him the helping hand he had awaited so many years.

Yes, it was Christ! Is that the reason, my God, why You became incarnate? Surely, we know it well; You came to take on our faults, and expiate them, but You also came to make God *present* to us, to be this presence Yourself—to strengthen, encourage, reassure, and calm. "Come to me, all of you. . . ." Is this why You worked the incomparable marvel of the Eucharist, the multiplication of Your Presence on earth, especially wherever there is a priest to say: "This is my body"?

To be everywhere at once is God's privilege alone. We poor men are imprisoned by time and space. For a noble soul, this is one of the saddest limitations. He wants to multiply his presence, knowing well that to be "all things to all men" is a beautiful ideal that can only be realized imperfectly.

At least, let him do what he can.

There are times when we must do even the impossible

to bring our presence to those who need joy or comfort. In times of great joy, for instance—at the sudden return of someone hopelessly absent for a long time. Our presence adds to that joy.

It is especially needed at moments of great sorrow. Sometimes we just do not think of it, or timidity holds us back. I remember receiving a visit, several years ago, from a tearful mother. This is what she told me: her only son had been called by God to religious life in a contemplative Order. No one around her had understood the greatness of this vocation, which people considered quite odd. On the day of his departure, there was no one there—none of her friends nor of her son's (and he was the member of a group where the word "fraternity" was not taken lightly). No one came to visit her or to keep her company. "You would have thought," she said, "that dishonor had befallen our house, or that my son had committed a crime."

To be there at the moment of a great parting, when a cruel sadness falls upon a family! To be there at tragic moments, when death is close! "I knew you would come," said a member of the underground, condemned to death by the occupation forces, to someone very dear to him. Yet Heaven knows what obstacles his friend must have had to overcome to be there. But he knew that his presence would be a blessing.

Have you ever waited for a visit—waited with all the strength of your being? And if that visit never came, you understand from what happened within you why you must never, without a grave reason, bring the same torment upon your friends.

A promise of a visit, especially to the sick who live in constant solitude, must be a sacred promise. Christ admirably brings out the importance of our presence near those who suffer. He promised His kingdom, not only for a glass of water given to the thirsty, but also for a visit made to the lonely: "I was a prisoner, sick, and you visited me...."

The mystery of another's presence! But we cannot always be there! Business, sickness, distance—all can keep us apart. Fortunately there are letters. Before becoming the tools of businessmen and diplomats, letters must have been the invention of love and charity. There is no doubt that they bring people together and increase their intimacy, at least as much as, if not more than, physical presence and conversation. All married couples who have been separated from one another by war and imprisonment understand this well.

There is among some, even among those very intimately united, an almost unconquerable timidity, that keeps them from revealing their hidden self and dealing with the essential subjects of life. It is continuous physical presence that sometimes makes deep harmony difficult and keeps souls from revealing themselves entirely.

If they find themselves separated, here is where letters can work a miracle. The lovers rediscover one another at a higher and more spiritual level. Essential topics are more easily brought up, without any neglect, however, of the trivial bits of news that are also a part of their lives.

War, as was said, has been the cause of a better understanding of these everyday truths. How impatiently prisoners wait for their mail!

"The magic of the postman," wrote one, "is stronger than ever. He is often late; and when we change our position, mail is sporadic and slow in arriving: forty-five, sometimes sixty days without a letter. When three weeks have gone by, life becomes twice as burdensome. What anxiety! Will it be today at last? That precious nourishment of a few lines on a piece of paper. Not yet, and still not yet. Lord, but it's tough!

"When it does come, you can't imagine my happiness to read of you. Don't change your tone; speak just as you always did. Talk of those trivial things, the news of everyone. Keep those mild and tender expressions of our total fidelity to each other. Let your letters bring home back to me, as they usually do. Believe me, it's simply breath-taking when, for a few moments, that little scrap of paper becomes home, *our* home in that familiar setting, the warm room, the children; those familiar acquaintances with their good and bad points, so intermingled that we have no choice but loving them as they are, or losing them completely; our smiling, bantering towns . . . you can't realize the value of these moments of escape."

Margeret Rivard, the foundress of "Auxilia," although an invalid, was a genius and had a keen insight into the human heart. She understood the miracle of letters very well. Her society is a flower of charity; and though it originated in France, it has spread in recent years into many other countries. Discreet, as genuine charity usually is, "Auxilia" is, however, not too well known.

Also called "Social Teams of the Sick," "Auxilia" organizes generous teachers who give lengthy correspondence courses to people who have been invalids for long periods, and especially to those suffering from tuberculosis. The idea behind these courses is to keep the invalid busy, to bring him out of his lethargy and boredom, and to prepare him to find later on an occupation in society suited to his state of health.

"Auxilia" is more than just a school. It requires the formation of real teamwork between teacher and pupil, a true friendship. It is not a question of pity that humiliates rather than helps. It is rather a drawing close, with all our powers of welcome, sympathy, and fraternity, to a brother who at present is in distress. What the invalid is seeking from the depth of his loneliness is obviously the possibility of preparing himself for a new profession, but it is *also* the presence of someone to whom he is no longer a stranger, labeled "tubercular," someone who proves this by faithfully adding a letter of true friendship along with the correspondence course.

If ever you have the free time, allow yourself the luxury of an altogether spontaneous and gratuitous letter. Suppose you learn some great sorrow has just struck a family you know, yet with whom you have not been in continual contact. Even if you do not receive an announcement of it, send a note of sympathy. It will be doubly welcome because it is unexpected.

But there are more than sorrows and trials in life; there are also joys. Success in examinations, an engagement or marriage, a birth, or some honor—there is no lack of opportunities for those who have a big enough heart. But to have this, we must flee from today's superficiality and reveal part of our soul.

26. *Work and Charity*

SOME people say: "Charity is for others. I'm so busy that I have no time in my life for the slightest gratuitous activity."

Are they sure of it?

Is it not true that one always finds time to do what one likes? Perhaps we just do not like doing things that bring us no return. It has often been shown that it is the busiest people who still find time for disinterested services.

Does this mean that we must not set aside time to rest, relax, pray, or develop our culture? Were this so, many people would wear themselves out in a few weeks. They could not give anything more to others because they would have a completely devitalized heart and soul. If we are to nourish others, we must also see to it that we are a substantial and nourishing food. But rare indeed are those who have really no time to devote to the slightest disinterested activity.

"Do not pretend frequently and without cause, either out loud or by letter, that you are too occupied," said Marcus Aurelius; "do not so continually shun your duties, imposed by social relations, under the pretext that you are overburdened by your own affairs."

"Love takes time," writes Dr. Tournier. "When one is

in a hurry, he never gives the impression of loving. Too
many social workers and priests are always in a hurry. So
it is that we admire their devotion, but sometimes doubt
their love. I am always struck by how tranquilly Christ
walked along the road, having time to chat with a lowly
woman beside a well, or answering the stupid questions of
His disciples on the eve of His passion. The spiritual ministry
takes a lot of time; and if one wishes to reserve some of it
for things more important than a soul, his ministry has become only a trade."

We should recognize, however, that many people lead
such a harassing life that they have only an infinitesimal
margin left for activities of pure devotedness. However, have
we forgotten that work itself is one of the great acts of charity? The material gain that comes from it has so overshad-
owed the other aspects of work that we have become blind
to its deep value and its prime essence. All activity (whether
mental or manual, practical or artistic) is a creator of good
and happiness, not only for oneself, but also for others.

Professions, in their infinite diversity, all are related to
one another, and make up, each in its own way, an ensemble
of services for the common good.

Work, then, *in itself,* in its profound reality, is a priv-
ileged place of exchange of love and communion. If only it
could become so *in fact!* If, instead of doing our daily job
with the spirit of a prisoner, we started each day with the
idea that we are going to place our stone in this great edifice,
and collaborate in the material welfare, the health, comfort,
security, intellectual enrichment, and spiritual development
of the whole community—what a change this would make
even in the most insignificant work! It would become a
beacon in our lives and warmth in our hearts.

We would all become a little like the mother who is busy from morning till night with her monotonous and simple tasks. She knows and feels that all her actions are necessary for the happiness of those for whom her heart is overflowing. This is how she can change those lowly and indispensable duties into a voluntary work that is full of love.

It is less easy for us to feel the same drive and warmth when we live outside the family circle. Only thought and meditation can develop in us a keener awareness of what we receive from the community and what we owe to it. The sense of the common good is too often placed in the background in our individualistic world. Still, in the words of Paul Claudel, "we form with our equals an ensemble of complementary organs, a body, a church. I need them all, just as they need me; and I receive from them an appeal that I cannot turn down."

There lies the redemption of work. It will never come solely from the outside. Even though many ameliorations ought to be continually sought for a more humane organization of work, it is from our interior attitude, from our heart and our love, that the salvation will come.

> . . . all work is empty save when there
> is love;
> And when you work with love you bind
> yourself to yourself, and to one another,
> and to God.

> And what is it to work with love?
> It is to weave the cloth with threads
> drawn from your heart, even as if your
> beloved were to wear that cloth.
> It is to build a house with affection, even

as if your beloved were to dwell in that
house.

It is to sow seeds with tenderness and reap
the harvest with joy, even as if your beloved
were to eat the fruit.

It is to charge all things you fashion with
a breath of your own spirit. . . .

Work is love made visible.

And if you cannot work with love but only
with distaste, it is better that you should
leave your work and sit at the gate of the
temple and take alms of those who work
with joy.

For if you bake bread with indifference,
you bake a bitter bread that feeds but half
man's hunger.

And if you grudge the crushing of the
grapes, your grudge distils a poison in the
wine.

And if you sing though as angels, and
love not the singing, you muffle man's ears
to the voices of the day and the voices of
the night.[1]

If, on the other hand, these same thoughts impregnate
our spirit, what respect and admiration we would have for
our brothers, what gratitude toward all those who work in-
cessantly for us; the architect and the mason who build our
homes, the weaver who makes our clothes, the farmer who

[1] Reprinted from *The Prophet* by Kahlil Gibran with permission of the publisher, Alfred A. Knopf, Inc. Copyright 1923 by Kahlil Gibran; renewal copyright
1951 by Administrators C.T.A. of Kahlil Gibran estate, and Mary G. Gibran.

gives us our bread. We would have to list here all the professions—the lowliest and the most brilliant—for we continually receive from them all that is necessary and luxurious, useful and agreeable.

One of the most evident signs of a cultured man of noble character is the esteem he has for the lowest of professions.

> The laborer said to me in a dream: "Make your own bread,
> I will feed you no longer; plow the earth and sow."
> The weaver said to me: "Make your own clothing."
> And the mason said to me: "Take up the trowel in your own hands."

The poet, Sully Prudhomme, has chosen the basic trades, those that give us bread, clothing, and lodging. But let us consider those tasks classed among the humblest.

Imagine, for instance, that no one wanted to do cleaning anymore, that the scrubwoman abandoned her mop, that the street-cleaner went on strike, and the highway department refused to work. After twenty-four hours, dust would be everywhere; and at the end of two days there would be no way to eat or drink; after a week, the atmosphere would be polluted; and in a month's time there would be a plague and cholera.

Yes, let us thank God for these people, and thank them for all they have done for us. We shall conclude with the poet, who said, upon waking from his dream and seeing everyone at work:

> I knew my happiness and I knew that no one in this world
> Can boast of surpassing men.
> And from that day on, I loved them all.

27. *Propaganda or Charity?*

THE apostolate ought to be the incarnation of a pure love of neighbor, the manifestation of a living charity.

Without a doubt the apostolate needs lectures, publications, organizations, manifestations, and certain propaganda. Our human condition demands that it be so. Nothing comes about in a purely spiritual way, even what is accomplished by the outpouring of the Holy Spirit. Propaganda is the obligatory liturgy of the apostolate. But like all liturgy, it risks forgetting its soul, becoming materialistic and hard, corrupting itself—a risk all the more dangerous since the mission of the apostolate is the highest a man can have. The soul of the apostolate is charity, sincere love of God and men; it is the burning desire to give the best one has to others, what he holds as the good *par excellence*: God, his life, his love, and all the light, security, force, and certainty his faith has given him.

Without the apostolate of love, the apostolate of propaganda is emptied of its life's blood. Instead of appearing as an appeal to non-Christians, it appears as a war machine, a challenge. The danger is especially threatening in the case of great public manifestations. These are easily taken for a haughty affirmation of self, boasting, a show of force, even when they have no other aim than displaying the purest and most fraternal of ideals.

The apostolate of propaganda easily looks upon men to win over as "numbers." It is busy with recruiting, counting numbers, loving figures and statistics. It says: "The congress of a hundred thousand," and risks forgetting the value or valuelessness of this crowd.

The apostolate of charity also takes into account the crowd, but there is first of all a sacred awe in the presence of persons, each individual, his case, his drama, and his destiny. It has a very vivid feeling of the unique value of each man and of the need to help all find the true life. It aspires to see all men become Christian, but it is not the number as such that interests it. Rather, its preoccupation is in seeing each brother adhere, by a truly inner, free, and personal act, to the Church, to Christ, and to God. It is not enough that one is baptized, that he is Catholic in name, that he votes for a party with Christian principles, nor even that he is enrolled in a Catholic Action organization or a religious sodality. Above all these, it is concerned with seeing men who are really and sincerely attached to God grow in number.

"Certainly, it is not a question (at least not primarily or uniquely, we would say) of increasing the number of members in the Church, or of recruiting great numbers of militants, or of organizing grandiose manifestations. Rather, it means opening the Christian way of life to men. It means aiding them to enter into Christian life more completely. It means helping them to begin giving themselves to God, or to give themselves to Him more deeply."[1]

When it is not rooted in an intense charity, the apostolate

[1] Yves de Montcheuil, S.J., *For Men of Action*, translated by Charles E. Parnell (Chicago: Fides Publishers, 1951).

of propaganda easily becomes a profession, a trade: one *works* at the apostolate as if he were spreading propaganda for a syndicate or political party. For some, apostolic activity becomes purely administrative. Or if they keep an apparent dynamism, it comes from a mania for activity, a need to speak and act and organize rather than a sincere conviction. So it is that we are amazed at certain propagandists turning Catholic Action into revolutionary social action. During the war, for example, some young Belgians joined forces with the Germans because they had been unable to reach England to join the allies. They dreamed only of fighting, and did not care whom they fought against.

The apostolate of charity is, above all, a sincere consecration of self to God. It requires an informed mind and a deep awareness of the mystery of Christ, of the human person, of sin and redemption, and of grace. And it flows from this awareness. It is this intimate conviction that one spreads and communicates. For he would like to share his discovery with all men.

If the apostolate of propaganda is not always animated by love and charity, it very quickly becomes a cold and official sort of collaboration purely for the outward development of a work, an organization, an ideology, or a system. And so it easily develops prejudices, changes into pure "opposition," and approaches a "crusade spirit" that dreams of exterminating the "adversary" rather than converting him. Father Pierre Charles, S.J., tells us how, in Argentina during a Catholic parade, he heard: "Long live Christ the King, and death to the Jews!" Here is an error that makes us shudder. "What we do *against* someone," writes Father Congar, O.P., "even *against* his error, for that matter, we do not do like a Catholic."

"As for me," said Elisabeth Leseur, "I am anti-Anti!"

The apostolate of charity is never opposition, but communion. There are no "adversaries" for it. Doubtlessly there are men in error or possessing only half-truths, but, far from showing any resentment, it knows only real love and sincere friendship for them. It would never judge their value in the eyes of God. Perhaps their ideal is purer than its own; perhaps they are closer to the divine truth than others who honor God with their lips, but live far from Him. The apostolate of charity does know, however, that it carries the whole truth, and is responsible for its diffusion among men. It in no way conceals the strong desire to see all men profess the same faith. But it uses no tricks on them, no deceits, no camouflages. It abhors the slightest dissimulation, the least insincerity. It simply and calmly presents, as best it can, the truth as it sees it, insisting upon the aspect of love, but without ever forcing arguments or hiding the stern demands of religion. It is glad to point out the half-truths professed by others and all that may bring them closer. It willingly believes in the sincerity of those who do not belong to its faith. It knows how to acknowledge that, even if the Catholic religion is to its mind the only completely true one, all Catholics and even some ecclesiastical institutions are not perfect. It bewails the faults committed by its brethren in the past and at present, and it deplores the evil that is caused by the sluggishness, bigotry, and sometimes scandalous conduct in the spreading of truth.

Propaganda naturally has for its role the orchestration of all outward means in the service of the truth. These means are somewhat related to what are called worldly grandeurs. It is a mass or number of treatises, newspapers, and reviews. It is the splendor of manifestations, the style of parades, the rhythm of marching, the songs, the scenic plays, bugle and trumpet. Propaganda takes money, for all these things are expensive. There is the financial support of organizations, the life of politics, the help of the state. Now all these things are surely legitimate, but their path is sown with ambushes. There is a great danger that a man will put his confidence above all in these rich means and become attached to the corrupt powers of this world, to organizations or movements that are not unimpeachable, to economic, social, or political structures devoted to destruction. This is why Pope Pius XII warns Christians to be on guard against "ostentatious action in magnificent public manifestations."

The apostolate of charity believes above all in "poor means," weak in the eyes of the world; that is, in faith, sincerity, purity, poverty, the spirit of truth, humility, and charity. It has confidence in the power of the Gospel; it believes, says Jacques Maritain, in the "vital energy of religion itself, in Faith operating more through Charity than through the Law. Here are the means, both poor and efficacious: We have been told to pray always. It is here that we must begin. Catholics know the efficacy of prayer, fasting, and works of penance and mercy. They have the sacraments, the intercession of the saints, public prayers, God's presence in them Who hears in secret. If they applied themselves to what they know by putting their heart and soul into the struggle, a great many things would change."

The apostolate of propaganda is likewise tempted to put pressure on people, exercise a moral restraint on their consciences, and exploit what is most spiritual in man to appeal to the instincts and passions, fear, aggressiveness, and frenzy dormant in every man. It is tempted to seduce men with base and selfish motives, almost without being aware of it, so great is its desire for visible success.

The apostolate of charity never forgets that the faith

and love with which one gives himself to God have value only inasmuch as they are really free. It aspires to orientate the liberty of man on its way to God, but it respects this liberty too much to lower itself by duping men with tricks that would amount to a moral swindling. The conduct of the apostle of charity "is not dictated by a care for human dignity alone, but also by a sense of the requirements of God. That which does not come forth from the innermost soul is of no value to the apostle, for God does not profit thereby. The whole idea of an apostolate where force enters is an absurdity to him.

"He refuses every form of constraint, even when subtly disguised. From the prestige of an eloquence which tries to snatch man out of himself to the charms of great and enveloping friendship, the ways of maneuvering a soul without seeming to do it violence are many. One may be able to handle a soul with consummate skill. But the apostle refuses himself anything which captivates the person, even when the latter is unaware of it, for he knows that God is thus deprived of the only thing which has any worth for Him: a free will which, in the fullness of its self-mastery, makes a gift of itself through love. This is the decisive factor.

"There are no infallible methods for bringing a free will to a decision. All tricks, all strings, all recipes are not only useless, because ineffective, but also ridiculous, because not connected to the goal to be obtained. They are thus odious, for they seem to do violence to the inner sanctuary of the soul. Finally, for those who see clearly they are sacrilegious, because they try to usurp a function which belongs to divine grace alone.

"To help someone who asks for support, however, to enlighten someone who asks for light (although even here one must be careful not to go beyond his role), to bring about the first step, the inner decision taken by a free will which is tearing itself from the attraction of evil or from inertia within imperfection in order to give itself over to love—this is quite another thing. Without a doubt much of our activity with others is spent in acting as a guide to those who already seek and those who wish to go still farther, but this is only a secondary function in the apostolate. The first step is to get others to decide to begin."[2]

Finally, the apostolate of propaganda, eager to succeed and tabulate its victories, risks discouragement when the results come in slowly. It even lets itself fall victim to impatience and bitterness and pour out haughty, ill-willed, and sarcastic remarks.

The apostolate of charity knows that a soul is not gained for God without enduring patience.

"We must behave as if we were standing before Christ in the Eucharist, and listen in peaceful and total contemplation of Him. We must wait with eyes lowered before the mystery of a soul, conquer the other's resistances by the force of our love, since he is usually refusing our love because he never met with love before.

"We must await a moment that may never come, keep a serenity that is not characteristic of man, cast the best of oneself into a void that may never be filled."

Never cut away what binds you together; never abandon a soul. Even if it abandons you and flees, stay near it with all the violence of your thwarted affection; keep it more than ever in the heart of your prayer! Never despair over anyone! Believe invincibly that your love and prayer will merit for the guiltiest of souls and the most prodigal of

[2] Yves de Montcheuil, *For Men of Action.*

children a saving light, be it only at the hour of their last breath.

Show a discretion that reflects God. "Every apostolic work ought to join to a total abnegation, a sort of indifference to the immediate results. This indifference is the absence of that haste which reveals complacency in work well done. Discretion: knowing when to speak and when to be silent; knowledge of the occasion and moment; acceptance of secondary causes and their infinite slowness; a zeal that knows how to appear like the very absence of zeal —what opportunities for a discreet spirit! Shall we be less patient than God?"

28. *More, Always More!*

"AH! LOVE is no laughing matter!"

Throughout these pages you must have grasped the truth in this verse of Marie Noël. Perhaps you have concluded that, "if charity demands so much, I'm not far along the way." It's very true: most of us are not very far on the way of love.

Even the saints did not believe they had reached the end. When Saint Vincent de Paul was asked by a nun what one should do to realize his vocation fully, he replied: "More, always do more!" This slogan should stick like an arrow in our heart all our life. We can, and we ought always, do more.

"By this shall all men know that you are my disciples," said Jesus, "if you have love for one another."

We hear much about this; we hear much preaching about charity. Pamphlets and books are written about it. More than that, men create works of charity, and Christians participate in them, giving their devotion, their time, and even their money. But not all! Not enough! Not in a pure enough way! And this is why our charity does not shine out, does not strike home. Moreover, we need not worry whether it shines forth or strikes home. All we need worry about is that it simply *be,* and that it never be content with itself.

This should be understood in two ways. The first concerns the effective realizations of charity. Who would dare pretend that he is going to the very limit of his means? Who would dare say he is dedicating all the time he can to his neighbor, all the money at his disposal? Who is cutting down on his expenditures and depriving himself so he can give away more? Who is exposing himself to a curtailed life to help a neighbor in great and at times extreme want? I know very well that only certain exceptional persons, and the saints, reach the end of the path of charity and the other virtues. I know that many others, at least, remain perpetually upset and discontent with their luxury, egoism, and stinginess. They really suffer from the distress of so many of their brothers. They conceal the temptation to an easier life. Year after year they are willing to take a risk to do more and more, and they sometimes give in to a generous act that is a little senseless. We all have too much fear of the follies of charity!

But besides the question of "quantity" there also arises the question of the "quality" of our charity. We all know what sarcasms Nietzsche voiced against Christian love. He calls it the "delicate flower of resentment." The love Christ preached is at heart a deceitful beating-around-the-bush held up to the weak and powerless to change weakness into merit and impotency into greatness. It is a moral for slaves. Standing up for those who could never be strong, rich, or powerful, Christianity has overturned the scale of values; it has depreciated strength, richness, and power to proclaim as blessed the poor, the meek, the patient, and humble.

"And the impotence which requites not, is turned to 'goodness,' craven baseness to meekness, submission to those whom one hates, to obedience (namely, obedience to one of whom they say that he ordered this submission—they call him God). The inoffensive character of the weak, the very cowardice in which he is rich, his standing at the door, his forced necessity of waiting, gain here fine names, such as 'patience,' which is also called 'virtue'; not being able to avenge one's self is called not wishing to avenge one's self, perhaps even forgiveness (for *they* know not what *they* do— we alone know what they do). They also talk of 'love of their enemies' and sweat thereby." So writes Nietzsche.

This is evidently a challenge. By means of a monstrous apriorism, Nietzsche affirms that Christian love can only have inferior and base motives. For him, always and in every instance, goodness can only be weakness, humility only fear, and patience only cowardice.

The feebleness of such a conception is shocking. Yet there is something in it to make us reflect. Nietzsche would have been closer to the truth if he had said that Christian love is so high a value that we almost never in our lifetime arrive at loving with perfect purity. We slide very easily from altruistic and disinterested to egoistic motives in our charity which make it impure and deceitful. It is true that sometimes people are patient just to avoid difficulties, or forgiving to avoid a scene, or good to make themselves popular, or generous out of pity rather than love.

What else can we say except that the very best things in man risk corruption, and that all the virtues constantly demand our watchfulness to keep them free from the corruptions that threaten them.

Christian love, more than any other virtue (for it is the highest of them all), needs to be orientated toward a gratuitousness that is absolute. We cannot love our neighbor for our own advantage, nor for that of a faction, country, religion, or church. We must love our neighbor because he is himself. We must love him in himself and in the One who is more present in him than he himself is: God.

Such is our Lord's command.

A NOTE ON THE TYPE

IN WHICH THIS BOOK WAS SET

This book has been set in Granjon, a lovely Linotype face, designed by George W. Jones, one of England's great printers, to meet his own exacting requirements for fine book and publication work. Like most useful types, Granjon is neither wholly new nor wholly old. It is not a copy of a classic face nor an original creation, but rather something between the two—drawing its basic design from classic Garamond sources, but never hesitating to deviate from the model where four centuries of type-cutting experience indicate an improvement or where modern methods of punch-cutting make possible a refinement far beyond the skill of the originator. This book was composed by Progressive Typographers, Inc., York, Pa., printed by Wickersham Printing Company of Lancaster, Pa., and bound by Moore and Company of Baltimore. The design and typography of this book are by Howard N. King.